IMAGES
of America

CHEVROLET
1911–1960

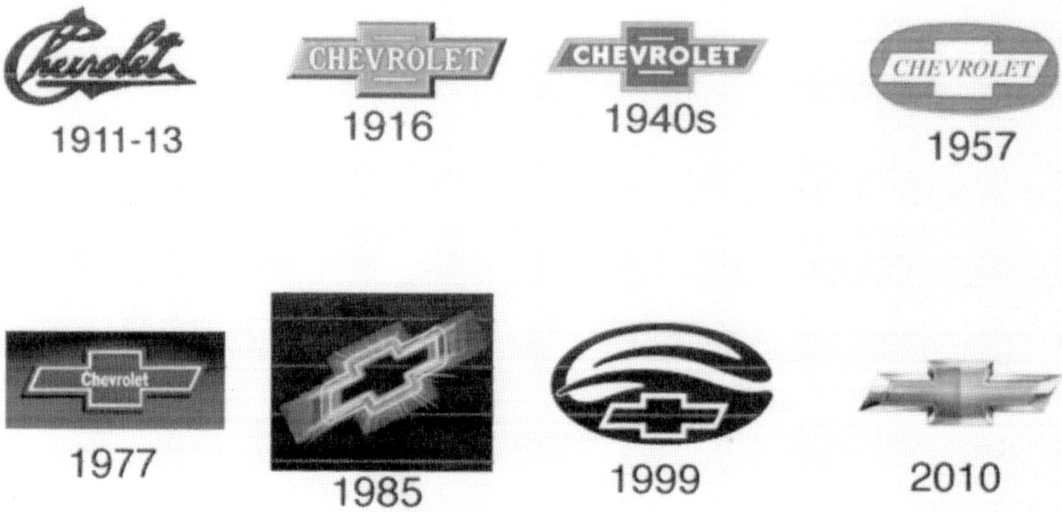

Chevrolet has not always used its iconic bowtie symbol as the vehicle's trademark, but it has been shown consistently through the years since the badge was first mounted on a 1914 Chevrolet radiator and used in advertising. Chevrolet and General Motors founder William C. Durant adapted the image from a newspaper advertisement for a coal product he saw while on vacation in Virginia. (Courtesy of General Motors Media Archives.)

On the Cover: Automotive history was made on January 11, 1940, when General Motors produced its 25-millionth production car, a 1940 Chevrolet sedan. Chevrolet and GM officials celebrated at the Chevrolet assembly plant in Flint, Michigan, including GM president and former Chevrolet general manager William S. Knudsen, with his hand on the fender. (Courtesy of National Automotive History Collection.)

IMAGES
of America

CHEVROLET
1911–1960

Michael W. R. Davis

ARCADIA
PUBLISHING

ISBN 978-0-7385-9394-4

Published by Arcadia Publishing
Charleston, South Carolina

Printed in the United States of America

Library of Congress Control Number: 2012939737

For all general information, please contact Arcadia Publishing:
Telephone 843-853-2070
Fax 843-853-0044
E-mail sales@arcadiapublishing.com
For customer service and orders:
Toll-Free 1-888-313-2665

Visit us on the Internet at www.arcadiapublishing.com

Contents

ACKNOWLEDGMENTS

As with a number of my past Arcadia Publishing photographic histories, the National Automotive History Collection at the Detroit Public Library ("N" in image credits) has been a major source of images for this history of Chevrolet. I am indebted to the following staff members of the library for their assistance: Mark Bowden, Dawn Eurich, Paige Plante, Carrie Pruett, and Robert Tate. Once again, Larry Kinsel of GM Media Archives ("G") has been patient and accommodating in his assistance with GM images.

Others who helped along the way include fellow automotive historians Terry Boyce and Jim Wagner; Jerry Burton, whose *100 Years of Chevrolet*, coauthored with Ralph Kramer, is a collector's gem; Flint historian Kevin Kirbitz ("K"); fellow author Larry Gustin; Ken Koleda of Genessee County ("C"); and automotive data expert Tom Libby; as well as GM staff experts Christo Datini, Scott Settlemire, Greg Wallace, and Tom Wilkinson. Heather Moore of the Sloan Museum ("S") and David White of the Kettering University Archives ("U") also were most accommodating. A "D" indicates my own images—either from my camera or my personal collection, including some images from various sources that were keyed in my previous Arcadia automotive histories.

As usual, my wife, Karen, bore up without much companionship from me during the intensive creation of this volume, and for its completion I am grateful for her patience and excellent copyediting skills.

BIBLIOGRAPHY

Automotive News, the 100-year Almanac. Detroit, MI: Crain Publishing, 1996.

Binder, Alan and Deebe Ferris, ed. *General Motors in the 20th Century*. Southfield, MI: Ward's Communications, 2000.

Burton, Jerry and Ralph Kramer. *100 Years of Chevrolet*. New Albany, IN: Automobile Quarterly Publications, 2011.

Davis, Michael W. R. *General Motors: A Photographic History*. Charleston, SC: Arcadia Publishing, 1999.

Gustin, Lawrence R. *Billy Durant, Creator of General Motors*. Grand Rapids, MI: Eerdsmans Publishing, 1973.

Gustin, Lawrence R. and Terry B. Dunham with the staff of *Automobile Quarterly Magazine. The Buick: A Complete History*. Sixth Edition. New York: American Heritage Publishing, 2002.

Gustin, Lawrence R. *David Buick's Marvelous Motor Car*. Second Edition. Flint, MI: Alfred P. Sloan Museum, 2011.

Kirbitz, Kevin M. *Before the Bowtie: Laying the Foundation for Chevrolet in Flint*. Flint, MI: Presentation to Vintage Chevrolet Club of America, July 20, 2011.

Sloan, Alfred P. Jr. *My Years with General Motors*. Garden City, NY: Doubleday & Co., 1964.

Standard Catalogue of American Cars, 1805–1942. First Edition. Iola, WI: Krause Publications, 1985.

Standard Catalogue of American Cars, 1946–1975. First Edition. Iola, WI: Krause Publications, 1987.

Standard Catalogue of American Light-Duty Trucks, 1896–2000. First Edition. Iola, WI: Krause Publications, 2001.

INTRODUCTION

Chevrolet's 100-year history nominally began November 3, 1911, when William C. Durant incorporated the Chevrolet Motor Company. Only three years earlier, Durant had founded General Motors. Having failed to enlist Henry Ford in General Motors—Durant's bankers wouldn't advance the upfront cash Ford wanted—Durant decided to launch Chevrolet as a low-priced car to compete with Ford.

As this new photographic history of Chevrolet's first 50 years (1911–1960) demonstrates, the company's roots actually go back another 60 years to Durant's grandfather Henry Crapo, who made a pile of money in New England's whaling industry. Crapo then invested his bankroll in 14,000 acres of timber in Lapeer County, east of Flint, Michigan, in the 1850s. Crapo's idea was to cut the timber and float the logs down the Flint River to a large sawmill in Saginaw, with easy access to Lake Huron freighters. When he found out logs could not be floated to Saginaw because of rapids in the river, he built his own sawmill above the rapids in Flint, counting on an existing railroad to deliver his lumber to lake shipping.

Soon there were many sawmills along the river in Flint. But in just a few more years, nearby forests had been largely cleared and sawmill operators turned their woodworking expertise to manufacturing horse-drawn vehicles. Among the 30 or so buggy-makers in Flint by the 19th century's end was the Durant-Dort Carriage Company, an 1886 partnership of Billy Durant and Dallas Dort that produced a remarkable 50,000 units in 1900. Durant conceived that achieving high volume sales success in buggy manufacturing required three coordinated tasks: (1) control of parts suppliers, (2) a strong network of sales and service dealers, and (3) clever promotion—business concepts that later led to the success of Chevrolet. However, it was rival Flint carriage manufacturer James Whiting who foresaw the need to invest in the new motorcars, bringing Buick from Detroit to Flint in 1904 and later inviting Durant to manage Buick.

By 1911, when Durant started Chevrolet, there were some 270 motorized vehicle brands on the US car market. Today, only four of those 270 American makes survive: Chevrolet, its sister General Motors brands Buick and Cadillac, and Chevrolet's longtime archrival, Ford.

In its first full year, 1912, Chevrolet managed to produce, at most, 2,999 units of its new car, the overpriced $2,150 Classic Six. That same year, Ford turned out 170,068 Model T cars in its American plants plus another 11,584 in Canada. Today, Chevrolet can state that more Chevrolets have been sold worldwide than any other brand. This is the story of that remarkable success.

When Ford shut down its factories in 1927 to convert from the legendary T to the Model A, Chevrolet outsold the pioneer mass-production leader for the first time, a prize it has maintained in the United States for most of the succeeding years of its 100-year history. Chevrolet accomplished this by following Durant's original concepts plus ingenious marketing, expanded production capacity, and notable engineering improvements under the guidance of GM greats Alfred P. Sloan Jr. and William S. Knudsen, the latter a former Ford production expert.

Chevrolet's first 50 years were arguably its most successful. Chevy overcame Ford's production and sales leadership in the 1920s, expanding that dominance in the 1930s, then made important but little-heralded contributions to the Arsenal of Democracy in the 1940s, and pioneered long-lasting product developments in the 1950s. In this final decade of its first 50 years, Chevy introduced new creature comforts such as automatic transmissions and power steering for the "low-priced" market followed by the Corvette sports car and the small-block V8 that ultimately propelled Chevrolet from its traditional value image to street-and-track high performance for the muscle car era of its second 50 years.

By the end of Chevrolet's first half-century, the manufacture of automobiles had grown enormously complicated with many layers of suppliers contributing to the final assembly. These suppliers began with raw materials (such as iron ore and paint ingredients), and progressed upward in the supply chain to parts making (such as tires and door handles), then to sub-assemblies (such as seating and transmissions). Any time a design was changed, whether mechanical or cosmetic, it could have repercussions throughout the supply chain. Thus by 1960, it could be said that the auto industry—in which Chevrolet was the largest producer—accounted for one out of every seven jobs in America.

I have never owned a Chevrolet or any other General Motors product. To top it off, I spent 25 years in public relations with Ford Motor Company, where General Motors was the enemy, the overwhelming competitor. The reader and Chevy enthusiast might well ask: what is a Ford guy doing with a book about Chevrolet history?

There are three interconnected reasons. First, Detroit is really a small town, a one-industry town—an automobile town. We metropolitan Detroiters may be work rivals, but we go to church with one another, our children go to school together, we serve on civic committees together, we play golf together—we are neighbors and friends. Like members of the different branches of the armed forces, there is fierce rivalry among us, but we also have learned to pull together as an industry. When one of us is hurt the other also feels some pain, and we share some delight in one another's successes. Not everyone around Detroit might agree, but that is my take after more than 50 years here.

Second, after retiring from Ford, I advanced from being a mere journalist and publicist with a couple of history degrees to an author-journalist specializing in automotive history with the advantage of inside knowledge about how "automotive sausage" is made.

Third, after producing several corporate automotive photographic histories published by Arcadia, it was time for a good car "brand" book to combine elements of solid industrial history with enthusiast books like those about Chevrolet's Camaro and Corvette. Chevrolet's centennial provides that ideal opportunity.

As a journalist who has covered the automotive industry for many decades, I have known many of the prominent personalities in the industry and participated in countless discussions with other journalists and industry figures about Motor City people, products, organizations, events, and trends. What may be history for scholars—largely documents about past events—I helped create or observed firsthand for nearly 60 years. Therefore, this book on Chevrolet, like my earlier Arcadia volumes, is my version of an important piece of automotive history, boiled down to what can be told through pictures and their captions.

Above all, with its year-by-year photographic advance through Chevrolet's first 50 years, this book becomes a useful "spotter's guide" for collector-car enthusiasts, most of whom today have little firsthand memory of Chevrolets built in the early decades. I have also included significant Chevrolet trucks in this volume. And we can look forward to a sequel Arcadia book: *Chevrolet: 1960–2013.*

—Michael W. R. Davis
Royal Oak, MI
February 20, 2012

One

Chevrolet's Flint Roots 1855–1911

Chevrolet founder William C. "Billy" Durant (1861–1947) poses here in the early 1900s. He joined with Dallas Dort in 1886 to form the Flint Road Cart Company. After accumulating a small fortune building buggies, Durant invested in the infant Buick Motor Company in 1904. Four years later, he leveraged Buick's success into the creation of General Motors from dozens of other parts and vehicle makers. Henry Ford agreed to join GM in 1908, but the deal fell through when bankers denied the cash needed. When financial reverses forced Durant from GM in 1911, he formed Chevrolet as a competitor to Ford, using Chevrolet's initial success to regain control of GM in 1916. (G.)

Harvesting Michigan's northern pine forests was a major economic activity in the middle of the 19th century. Trees were cut down and sawn into convenient log lengths for transportation by rail or waterway to sawmills, where boards could be cut to build homes in Great Lakes cities such as Chicago, Cleveland, Detroit, Milwaukee, and Toledo. (D.)

Henry Crapo, Billy Durant's grandfather, came from Massachusetts in 1855 with money from the maritime industry to invest in lumber. He bought 14,000 acres of timber in Lapeer County, planning to float the logs down the Flint River to a sawmill in Saginaw. But rapids blocking the river below Flint forced him to build his own sawmill in Flint, shown along the river on the right (north) side in the lower center of this 1867 "birds-eye" illustration. The view faces southwest toward the Saginaw Street Bridge. (S.)

Following the Civil War, some of Flint's sawmill operators turned to buggy-making. Here, around 1900, a buggy (center rear) undergoes "bench-built" construction in a shop that also made bicycles and primitive motorcycles. Horse-drawn carriages, buggies, wagons, and carts were made of wood with metal hardware. (U.)

The buildings shown in this photograph from around 1890 constituted the Flint Wagon Works, owned by Durant's buggy-making competitor James H. Whiting. These buildings were converted to produce Whiting cars in 1911. After producing the Little car, the site became one of Chevrolet's first plants and offices when the company moved from Detroit to Flint late in 1912. (K.)

Blue Ribbon models of buggies produced by Durant-Dort Carriage Company are shown here at a "showroom" under a county or state fair tent around 1900. Note the similarity to today's promotional banners at automobile dealerships. At that time, Michigan was a mecca for producers of railroad cars, marine engines, cast-iron stoves, bicycles, and buggies, creating a pool of skilled workers and manufacturing plants to support the infant automobile industry. (D)

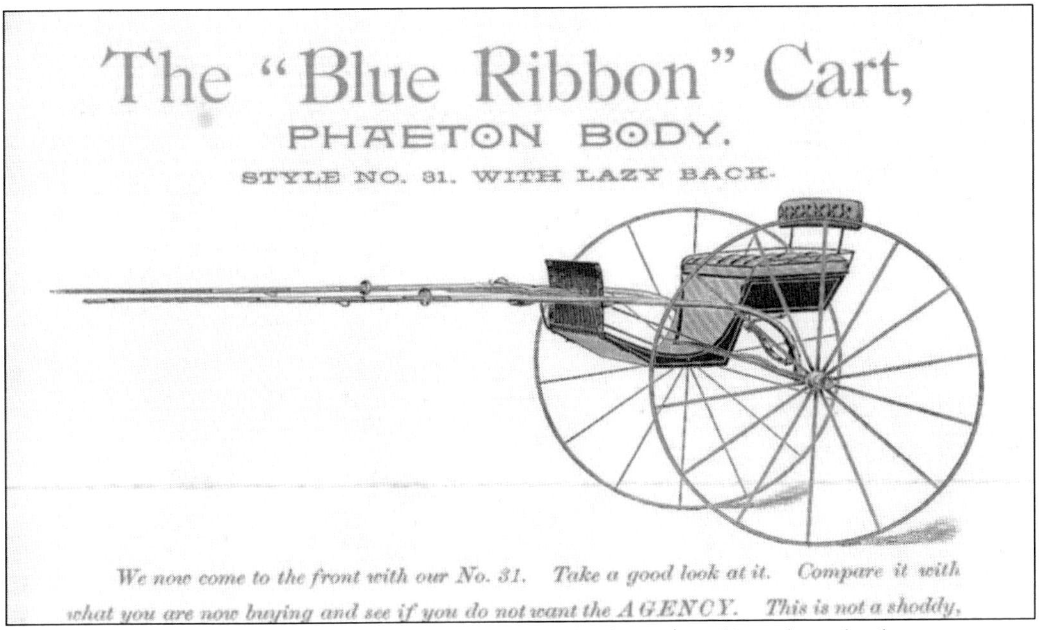

The simple Durant-Dort "Road Cart" sold for as little as $12.50 and made the two young Flint entrepreneurs wealthy in only a few years. It was the sports car of its time, lightweight with a spring suspension for fast travel behind a willing horse. Durant-Dort produced some 50,000 vehicles in 1900, a large share of them Road Carts like the slightly upscale cart in this catalogue illustration. (K.)

A competitor of Durant-Dort was W.A. Paterson, credited with pioneering Flint's buggy business in 1869. This image shows an array of newly assembled Paterson buggies, carriages, and carts ready for delivery to customers or shipment to distant points. Like other buggy factory owners around 1900, Paterson realized that the success of the infant automobile business spelled trouble for horse-drawn vehicles. (U.)

Through the successful development of buggy manufacturing, which combined an abundance of lumber, a pool of skilled woodworkers, and new metal-working shops for making buggy hardware such as axles and springs, Flint claimed the "Vehicle City" title for its Golden Anniversary in 1905, proclaimed by this sign over Saginaw Street. Similar signs still hang here today on what was the main north-south road through town. There were more than 30 buggy-making firms in Flint between 1850 and 1900. (D.)

Around 1900, James H. Whiting, the president of Flint Wagon Works, decided to get into the motor and motorcar business. He bought into the infant Buick Motor firm of Detroit in 1903 and within a year had persuaded Durant to invest in Buick, which Durant soon took over. (N.)

Buick's chief engineer, Walter L. Marr (left), and Thomas D. Buick, the son of Buick founder David Buick, were photographed here in the first Flint-made Buick as it ended a successful Flint-Detroit roundtrip over primitive roads in July 1904. (D.)

The first Flint Buick factory, shown here on West Kearsley Street near the Flint Wagon Works south of the Flint River, was originally one story in 1903 before expanding. At the time, it was located in a neighborhood of buggy factories and one-time sawmills. Railroad sidings were critical for plant locations to facilitate shipment of parts supplies in and finished automobiles out to markets. (K.)

A sporty Billy Durant (left) is shown in his fashionable visored cap. In most photographs outdoors, he is shown wearing a more formal bowler hat, but he likely would don this to attend an automobile race to observe Louis Chevrolet behind the steering wheel of a Buick, to promote the car's performance in the popular auto races of the time. William H. Little (right) was the Buick plant manager when production rose from 37 in 1904 to 30,525 in 1910, not far behind Ford's 34,859. In 1911, Durant designated him to be president of the new Little Motor Car Company in the former Flint Wagon Works, which Durant bought from Whiting. Little also became one of the incorporators of Chevrolet later that year. (Both, K.)

Louis Chevrolet was a famous Swiss-born racing driver, hired by Durant to race Buick cars and demonstrate their speed and reliability. Subsequently, Durant asked Chevrolet to design a new car to fulfill Durant's ambition to challenge Henry Ford's Model T. He decided to name the new car "Chevrolet" for marketing reasons. (K.)

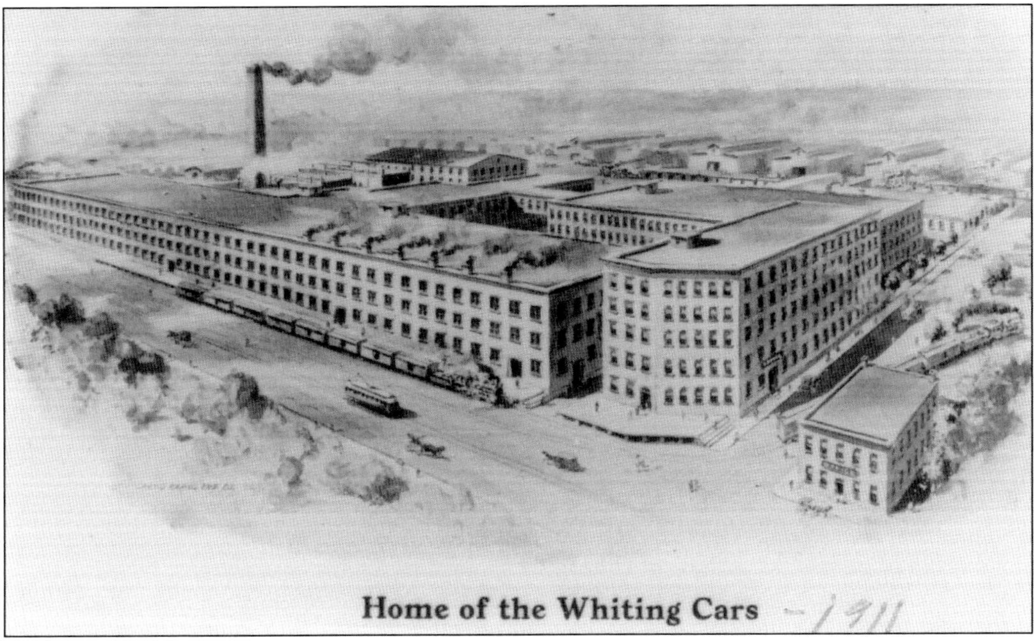

This early 1911 illustration of the former Flint Wagon Works is labeled "Home of the Whiting Cars" although it was still producing horse-drawn carriages, buggies, wagons, and carts as well. It was south of the Flint River on the west side of Flint, near the location of other buggy factories and supplier plants and—decades earlier—sawmills. (K)

This is the same artist's rendering of the Flint Wagon Works and Whiting automobile home shown on page 11 and above, now identified as "Home of the Little Four car." Durant owned all three companies and the factory building as he maneuvered to bring his Chevrolet to market. Auto historians have had a difficult time sorting out Durant's moves because of scarce documentation. (K.)

This display of Whiting cars has the Flint Wagon Works name prominently displayed. They were "medium-priced" and produced for three seasons only, from 1910 to 1912. Here, a saucy white roadster, or runabout, is in the center, flanked on either side by touring cars. Wheelbases ranged from 90 to 116 inches, horsepower from 20 to 40, and prices from $650 to $1,700. (N.)

On the northeast side of Flint, on the opposite bank of the Flint River, Imperial Wheel (above) was a major supplier to the buggy industry. Imperial had been established along with other buggy component suppliers by Durant-Dort. This facility morphed into a Chevrolet office and plant (below) briefly when Durant moved Chevrolet from Detroit to Flint in 1912. (K.)

Later, the Imperial-Chevrolet building shown on the previous page became home to other Durant ventures: Monroe Motor Company (above) in 1914 and, finally, Buick Motor Company (below) in 1916. After 1910, Buick erected complete vertically-integrated manufacturing facilities alongside the old Imperial building. The Imperial-Chevrolet-Monroe-Buick building was demolished in 1939. (K.)

This aerial photograph of Flint's Buick Motor Company factories, taken around 1938, shows how extensive the complex was, years before World War II and postwar expansion made it even larger. The circle pinpoints the Imperial Wheel-Chevrolet-Monroe-Buick building shown on the preceding two pages. The Flint River can be seen in the lower right corner. In the 1980s, the famous Buick City was created around this giant manufacturing complex. The historic plants were demolished after 2001 due to GM's financial woes and accompanying reorganizations. (K.)

Louis Chevrolet poses at the wheel of a 1910 Marquette-Buick racer. Note that the bucket seat is labeled with his name. Durant thought the name Chevrolet sounded French and—at a time when many pioneer US auto industry terms, such as "automobile" and "chassis," were French in origin—would therefore make a good name for a new motorcar. Decades later, Chevrolet advertisers found it also worked well for rhyming jingles, as in "See the U.S.A. in your Chevrolet." (K.)

This $690 1912 Little roadster, shown in a Chevrolet Centennial display at Flint's Buick Gallery of the Sloan Museum, became a Durant-orchestrated link between the earlier Whiting car and the 1914 Chevrolet Royal Mail roadster. Work on the car began in 1911 and the make was merged into Chevrolet in 1914. (D.)

Two

THE DURANT YEARS 1912–1920

This 1912 photograph of the prototype Chevrolet Classic Six shows Louis Chevrolet's design, a 3,500-pound touring car with a six-cylinder engine, priced at $2,150—far from what Durant had in mind to compete with Henry Ford's $690 Model T. Durant stands in the front row at the far right and Louis Chevrolet is in the white duster second from left. Durant's son, Cliff, is at the wheel. Other executives in the photograph include A.B.C. Hardy, later Chevrolet general manager, and William H. Little, head of the Little Motor Company, soon to be merged with Chevrolet. (N.)

This is the earliest Chevrolet known to still exist in the United States: body number 323, a 1913 Classic Six, at Flint's Sloan Museum. Note that the windshield mounting is different from the 1912 prototype on the previous page. There is an older, unrestored Classic Six at a museum in Canada. The car featured a 299-cid engine of 40 horsepower. (D.)

The Chevrolet offices at the former Flint Wagon Works are seen here shortly after the company was moved from Detroit in late 1912. This building can be identified at the right in three earlier images of the factory complex on pages 11 and 17. At that point, Chevrolet had two operations in Flint, here on the west side and also in the northeast (page 19). (K.)

Misguided Fisher Body promoters paraded around a bogus "1913" Chevrolet with a bowtie badge on its radiator, but bowties were not adopted by the company until 1914. This phony "First Chevrolet" is displayed at an auto show or dealership and is thought to be a 1914 Light Six or possibly a similar Little Six rather than a 1913 vintage Chevrolet, because only the Classic Six (pages 23 and 24) had been built at the time. (N.)

This group of models or reenactors, clad in vintage costumes, pose with the bogus "First Chevrolet." The staged photographs were taken in 1958, probably as part of GM's 50th anniversary celebration, and featured the models in a variety of street scenes with 1913-type buildings and even an occasional horse and buggy as props. (N.)

Chevrolet's bowtie emblem finally made it onto the car in this catalogue or advertising illustration of a 1914 Light Six, available only as the touring car shown. The bowtie logo is displayed both on the radiator and separately beside the car. Elsewhere, an advertisement proclaimed: "Pronounced Shev-Ro-Lay." (N.)

This advertisement is for the $750 1914 Royal Mail roadster, a descendant of the Whiting and Little cars. On this car and the companion $875 Baby Grand touring car (page 29) the Chevrolet overhead-valve (OHV) engine was introduced, albeit a Four rather than the later Six. The new Chevrolet design was adapted from earlier Buick motor designs of similar configuration. (N.)

This is a catalogue illustration for a 1914 Little Four. Its resemblance to the Chevrolet Royal Mail (opposite page) is clear, except for the lamps on the cowl. This was the last year for Durant's "other" small car, produced to compete with the Ford Model T, which was by then being mass-produced on a moving assembly line when other cars were still bench-built like buggies. (N.)

This contemporary 1915 photograph shows a Chevrolet Royal Mail roadster. Its 171-cid displacement Chevrolet engine was rated at 24 horsepower, compared to the similarly designed 1915 Buick OHV Four of 165 cid. Arthur C. Mason's Durant-owned motor company manufactured both Chevrolet engines—the Four and the earlier Six—in Flint. Mason had been an engine builder in Detroit and moved to Flint with David Buick. (N.)

Shown here is a restored 1915 Royal Mail owned by The Henry Ford museum in Dearborn, Michigan. When compared to the original on the preceding page, the most apparent difference is the all-white tires common before the white-sidewall tires such as these on the restored vehicle were invented. (N.)

Another variation on the 1915 Royal Mail is this rare coupe, created by attaching a hard top to the roadster body. It is not known if the top was removable as with Corvettes and other more recent sports cars. The coupe version, however, loses the sporty appeal of the roadster. A coupe model is not listed in the *Standard Catalogue* as being among 1915 Chevrolet models. It may have been either experimental or an aftermarket accessory offering. (N.)

This Chevrolet Baby Grand was the touring car body version of the Royal Mail. Durant's knack for marketing is evident in the appealing names given to the two models. Other than the coupe of uncertain provenance pictured on the previous page, Chevrolet offered only open cars from 1914 to 1916. According to the *Standard Catalogue*, the wheelbase of the 1915 models was up two inches to 106 inches. (N.)

This 1915 Baby Grand, on display in the Buick Gallery of the Sloan Museum, is parked alongside a 1920 490 Series touring car. The Baby Grand, like other touring cars of the time, comfortably provided seating for five adults. In cold weather or rain, however, motoring was anything but comfortable. Chevrolet tackled that issue with one of its 1917 models (page 34). (D.)

As Chevrolet sales increased dramatically in 1915, Durant lowered prices by introducing a new model to compete directly with the $490 Model T: this Chevrolet "490," the name denoting the price. Ford responded by lowering his touring car price to $440 in what was perhaps the opening gun in the century-long Motor City competition. (N.)

In 1915, when sales totaled 20,158 cars, Chevrolet also offered this sporty $985 Amesbury (referred to as Annenburg in some sources) Special roadster in white with wire wheels when other cars typically had wooden, buggy-like "artillery" wheels. By then, Durant had expanded production by leasing factories in New York City and St. Louis and buying a plant from Maxwell in Tarrytown, New York. Chevrolet of Canada was incorporated September 23, 1915. (N.)

This illustration from a 1915 Baby Grand catalogue shows the chassis—frame, suspension, and powertrain—of the 106-inch wheelbase and the OHV four-cylinder engine in the long-lasting front-engine, rear-drive configuration. Durant used Chevrolet profits to buy General Motors stock and regained control of GM in early 1916. (N.)

In late 1913, frustrated that Durant had not accepted his Chevrolet Classic Six design, Louis Chevrolet left Durant's employment and returned to racing, where he was very successful. Here he is posing at the wheel of a Cornelian racer at the 1915 Indianapolis 500. (N.)

Chevrolet Instrument Board and Control Devices—Everything Accessible, Easily Reached and Understood.

The image at left is from a Chevrolet sales booklet and shows the relatively simple instrument panel of a 1916 Royal Mail. Below is a photograph of a virtually unchanged 1920 Chevrolet 490 instrument panel in the Sloan Museum. Compare these to instrument panels of later-model Chevrolets shown on subsequent pages. (Left, N; below, D.)

This 1917 Chevrolet 490 sedan had an unusual body type at a time when most cars were either two-passenger roadsters or five-passenger touring cars. Chevrolet called these "all-season" models. It was priced initially at $1,060 "at the factory"—shipping charges to the sales point were extra. In 1917, Chevrolet sales saw a huge increase, to 109,115, but Ford sold 824,488. (N.)

The Allies of Britain, France, Italy, and Russia had been fighting the Central Powers of Germany, Austria, and Turkey for nearly three years when the United States joined the war on the Allied side. Here, a Chevrolet touring car driven by a Navy petty officer parades with a sign seeking enlistments in the US sea service. (N.)

At left, a man sits in the rear seat of a Chevrolet FA sedan, which was larger than the 490. Note the easy access via the single right-hand door, even without a folding-forward right front seat. Also, the flat floor of the 1917 car is a double-step down to the ground. At right, the gentleman in the rear seat stows the removable pillars—the "B" and "C" pillars in modern automotive usage—under the seat. Automobile bodies were still made of wood then, as were the horse-drawn carriages they were rapidly replacing. (N.)

This all-weather sedan has been transformed into a pillarless "hardtop" sedan similar to the body styles Chevrolet and other General Motors makes introduced between 1949 and 1956, which were soon copied throughout the domestic industry. (N.)

This is the closed, or "all-season," model offered by Chevrolet in 1917–1918, the $1,475 FA Series Touring Opera Car. It is identical to the model on the opposite page except that the pillars are attached. The FA Series had a 108-inch wheelbase, six inches longer than the 490. (N.)

The $1,550 1918 Series D Chevrolet Touring Car was notable for its 288-cid OHV V8 engine, which produced all of 36 horsepower. It was offered only one year before withdrawal. It was mounted on a 120-inch wheelbase and was Chevrolet's only V8 model until introduction of the 1955 "small block" V8s. Note that the cowl lines up straight with the hood, another distinction of the D Series from the 490 and F Series. (G.)

The closed cars Chevrolet now offered lacked the fresh-air ventilation of topless roadsters and touring cars. In response, Chevrolet introduced this openable, horizontally split windshield for its new FA Series sedan in 1917–1918. In effect, it was a predecessor of the artificial air conditioning that became an option 40 years later and is standard today. (N.)

This 1919 Chevrolet negotiates an unpaved country road and passes a Conservation Commission sign warning about careless fires. It symbolizes the grand transformation of American roads about to take place. The first concrete mile had been poured only a decade earlier, in Detroit, but cross-country driving, as well as simple joyriding, demanded paved, marked routes. The US highway system, financed with gasoline taxes, was only a few years away. (N.)

As motoring became more pleasurable, with easier electric starting and more reliability through other product improvements, driving appealed more to women. Previously, it had been a largely male occupation, often requiring mechanical skills for repairs. This woman drives a Chevrolet sedan along a scenic river or lakeside in 1919. (N.)

In 1918, an important and lasting introduction for Chevrolet was its first truck, or "commercial car," as such work vehicles were called into the 1960s. The first Chevy trucks were offered in a half-ton model based on the 490 and a beefed-up one-ton model called the Model T. This model appears to be a one-ton model with "canopy express" body. (N.)

The 1920 Chevrolet, sitting atop streetcar tracks, symbolized another upheaval in American urban travel: the displacement of electric streetcars and interurbans by automobiles. From 1910 to 1920, total US car sales grew from 173,406 to 1,432,655, and the future of local rail transportation was in doubt. Many streetcar and interurban companies went bankrupt in the 1920s due to the public's preference for private automobile transportation. (N.)

In 1919, Chevrolet introduced a new family of larger, more expensive FB Series cars, upscale from the continuing 490 line. Shown here is the least expensive model for 1920, the $1,210 FB 20 Roadster. Compared to the 490, FBs had a longer, 110-inch wheelbase and a larger, 224-cid, 37-horsepower OHV four-cylinder engine. (N.)

Another style in the FB Series was this 1920 "five-window" $1,795 FB 30 coupe, rated to carry three occupants. Coupes became a very popular body type with American motorists through the 1940s. The FB Series also included "40" sedan and "50" touring models as well as the "20" and "30" shown on this page. Throughout this period and up to the mid-1930s, new models were announced in the fall for introduction at auto shows in January. (N.)

Both already under Durant's control, Chevrolet and General Motors were merged on May 2, 1918, with Durant, shown here at his desk, continuing as president. But the master salesman, dealmaker, and marketer extended personal and corporate finances too far and was forced to resign from the General Motors presidency and board effective December 1, 1920. Durant had established what became the world's largest industrial corporation—and then lost it. (G.)

Three

The Knudsen Years 1921–1933

Seated here at his desk is William S. Knudsen, a Danish immigrant and bicycle mechanic and machinist who became a master of mass production at Ford in the mid-1910s but resigned in 1921 when he felt unappreciated by "Old Henry." GM Vice President and Director C.S. Mott hired him as a manufacturing assistant on February 1, 1922, and within a month, he was transferred to Chevrolet as production vice president. By the end of the year, Knudsen was head of Chevrolet. (G.)

GM's management knew if Chevrolet were to challenge Ford for sales leadership, it would have to match Ford's production capacity. In 1919, even before Knudsen's arrival, this all-new Chevrolet assembly plant on the west side of Flint was under construction. In 1921, reflecting the post–World War I recession, Chevrolet produced only 61,717 vehicles to Ford's approximately 870,000. A GM management survey recommended discontinuing Chevrolet. (G.)

One of the bright spots in Chevrolet's outlook for 1922 was the emerging market for light trucks with special bodies made by outside manufacturers, such as this panel-bodied one-ton Chevrolet Model T. Chevrolet light truck sales were about 7,100 in 1922, but by the end of the decade they had reached 161,000 annually. (N.)

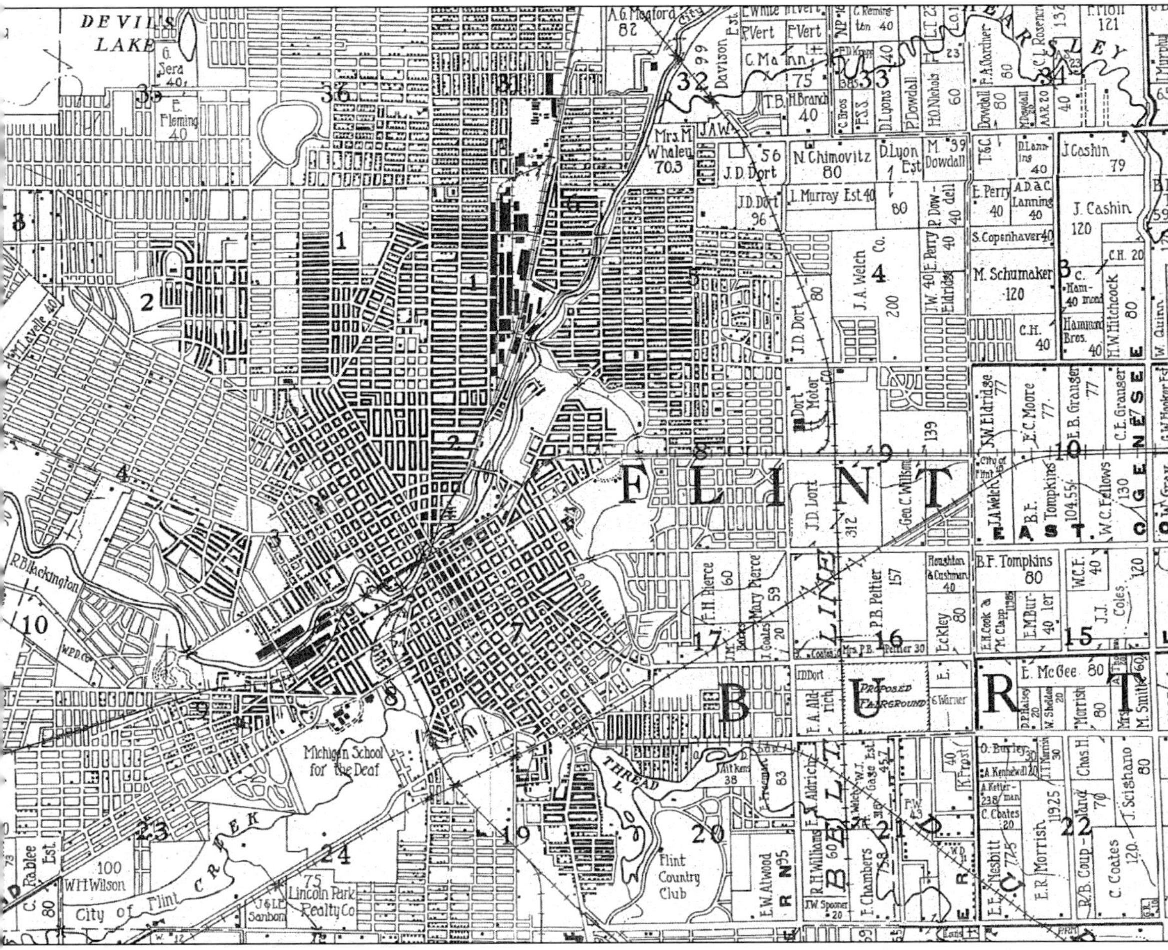

This 1924 map of Flint, Michigan, shows the opposite areas of the city where the two car lines, Chevrolet and Buick, had their main manufacturing operations. Chevrolet is south of the Flint River and west of the town center, where the main north-south road, Saginaw Street, crosses the Flint River. Buick is on the northeast side, on the opposite bank of the river. Later, Chevrolet expanded to the north side of the river. (C.)

Unfortunately, Chevrolet was burdened in 1923 by the disaster of its misbegotten copper-cooled engine. This 1923 Chevrolet Series M (copper-cooled) Utility Coupe had a unique non-radiator grille. Only 759 air-cooled engine cars were built and all but two were recalled and scrapped. The design had been developed at GM's Dayton Engineering Laboratories without extensive production validation or vehicle testing by Chevrolet engineers, and Chevrolet management was excluded from the corporate decision to introduce the then-radical feature. (N.)

The 1923 copper-cooled Chevrolet required a new chassis to accommodate its radical engine. This is a side view of the frame, engine, and other components normally hidden from view by the car body. With a clunker in the midst of an industry boom year of four million car and truck sales, Chevrolet fortunately was able to satisfy demand with its new Superior Series B. (N.)

Above is a cutaway illustration of the copper-cooled engine. Each of the four cylinders of the 22-horsepower, 135-cid engine was wrapped in copper shrouds. The fan in the upper right, driven by a belt from the crankshaft at the bottom, was supposed to cool the engine by blowing cool air from outside over the cylinders, where engine heat is generated by friction of the pistons moving up and down. This prospective airflow is shown in the diagram below. If it had worked, there would have been no threat of a radiator boiling over in hot weather or freezing in cold weather. (N.)

STAIR-STEP MARKETING

General Motors Prices

Make		August 1, 1922	Make	October 1, 1923
Chevrolet	"490"	$ 510 — $ 860	Chevrolet	$ 490 — $ 795
	"FB"	865 — 1395		
Buick	4	865 — 1395	Oldsmobile 6	750 — 1095
	6	1175 — 2195		
Oakland		975 — 1545	Buick 4	935 — 1495
Oldsmobile	4	1095 — 1745	Oakland	945 — 1395
	8	1495 — 2145	Buick 6	1275 — 2285
Cadillac		3100 — 4600	Cadillac	2985 — 4600

This table shows how GM initiated "stair-step" marketing by readjusting prices and model selection between the 1922 and 1923 models. With added-value features to justify ascending price classes, a ladder was provided with minimal overlap from Chevrolet to Cadillac, designed to keep the upwardly mobile in the GM family. This evolving price-and-product strategy was supplemented by other GM sales support activities, such as the General Motors Acceptance Corporation (GMAC) to finance dealer operations and retail purchases by customers. (D.)

In 1921, Chevrolet headquarters moved from Flint to this long five-level office building along Detroit's Milwaukee Avenue on the south side of the General Motors Building fronting West Grand Boulevard. It survived as Chevrolet's main office until 1979, when Chevrolet moved to a new building on Van Dyke Avenue, part of the GM Tech Center in Warren, Michigan, north of Detroit. After GM acquired Detroit's Renaissance Center from Ford in 1996, Chevrolet central offices returned to Detroit. (G.)

As the product part of its campaign to overtake Ford, Chevrolet introduced distinctive appearance upgrades, such as the disc wheels, bright-metal radiator shell, headlamp bezels, and bumpers seen in this Detroit street scene. This $695 1924 Chevrolet Superior Series F shows off the new two-door Coach body. Coach bodies went on to become the preferred automobile body type for American families in succeeding decades. (N.)

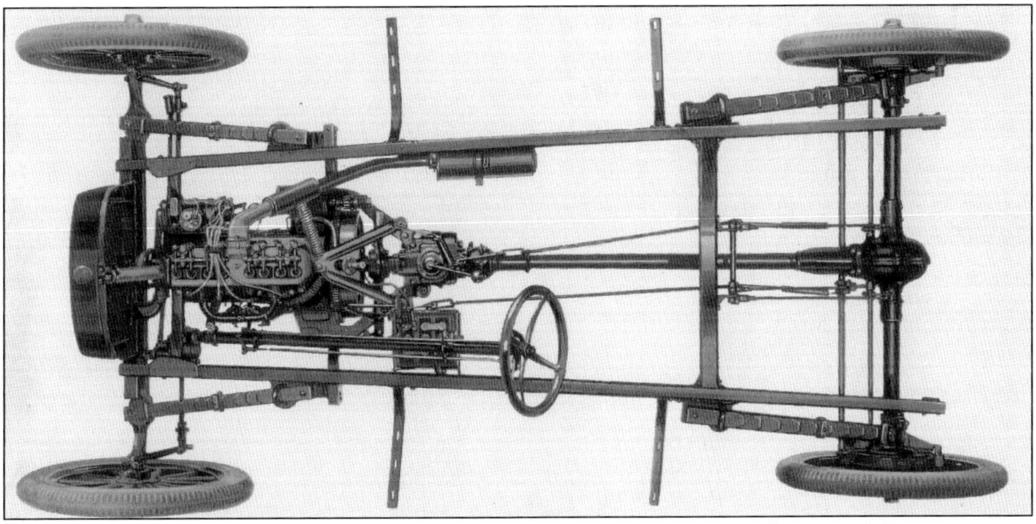

This is a "plan view" of the new frame for 1924 Chevrolets. Note that the top of the engine was open, exposing the rocker arms, unlike the arrangement with a valve cover seen in the 1915 chassis illustration on page 31. Also, the frame was more tapered to the front. The 1924 transmission housing was separated from the rear of the engine, though not as much as in 1915. The wheelbase of the 1924 was 103 inches, three less than in 1915, while the engine produced 26 horsepower, two more than the 1915. (N.)

Another Detroit street scene shows a 1924 Chevrolet panel truck delivering grocery items to a market. This Superior Series H half-ton truck was mounted on a 103-inch wheelbase—the same as the car—with a 171-cid OHV Four of 22 horsepower, less than the passenger car's engine. Combined Chevrolet car and truck sales rose to 321,000 for the year, still far behind Ford's 1,587,000. (N.)

Chevrolet introduced its new Superior K series for 1925. Production changes from the 1924 version took place on August 1, 1924—customary timing in the years before formal model years were established. Chevrolet also assembled its two-millionth vehicle, shown here in a publicity photograph. Chevrolet combined car and truck new registrations in 1925 reached 388,329, a modest increase over the prior year. (N.)

This small bus on a Chevrolet commercial one-ton truck chassis is shown in 1925 with a load of adult passengers, perhaps being used by a church or civic group. The same configuration could be used for urban feeder bus lines or school buses. Vehicle manufacturers relied on outside body companies to mount such bodies on bare chassis made at automotive assembly plants. (N.)

This is the standard 1925 Chevrolet OHV 171-cid, 26-horsepower four-cylinder engine and three-speed sliding-gear transmission, which powered Chevrolet cars since the 1914 models, with improvements along the way. In 1925, the automaker touted the fact that all components were "enclosed and protected from the weather," an improvement over earlier Chevrolet engines. (N.)

Following the copper-cooled Chevrolet crisis of 1922–1923, General Motors established the auto industry's first "scientific" proving ground in Milford, Michigan. This 1925 Chevrolet is having its brakes tested on a laboratory rig at the proving ground that allows more precise, repeatable, and thorough monitoring than brake-testing on the road. (N.)

This is a 1926 Chevrolet one-ton stake truck, which could be utilized for either commercial or agricultural purposes. Upon receiving an order from a dealer, Chevrolet would build a chassis, consisting of the frame, suspension, wheels, engine-transmission-drive axle, and front-end sheet metal and fenders, then ship it to a truck body builder for completion into the desired work truck configuration like the one shown. (N.)

Many variations of body designs were typical in the 1920s. This is a 1926 Chevrolet roadster with a trunk compartment for securely carrying luggage. The same rear space could accommodate a rumble seat in upscale roadster (page 53) or coupe models, or as shown below, for cargo carrying. In 1926, Chevrolet sales totaled 546,015 to Ford's 1,329,711, but Ford was about to hand its rival the leadership. (N.)

The same roadster body shown above is seen here with a farm wagon-like cargo area in the luggage space. Effectively, this 1926 Superior Series V roadster was a forerunner of passenger-car-based pickup trucks, culminating in the stylish El Camino models introduced in 1959 and continued into the mid-1980s. Such car-truck models have also been popular in Australia, where they are known as "utes" for their combination of comfort, economy, and utility. (N.)

This photograph of two fashionable females in the styles of the time shows popular upscale residential architecture—Colonial-style here—along with the car. The four-door sedan is a 1926 Superior Series V with a distinct two-tone paint scheme. DuPont laboratories devised Duco fast-drying automotive paint early in the decade and GM's new Art and Color Section applied the color choice variety to enhance sales appeal. (N.)

General Motors' far-flung industrial diversity, with many different high-technology businesses, created safe markets for GM's automotive division sales. Here, a fleet of Chevrolet coupes and trucks, arranged with the newest in front, are parked outside a facility of GM's Frigidaire refrigerator division. (N.)

This facsimile of a circus train locomotive and passenger car was used as a ticket office and bandwagon for the Morris and Castle Circus in 1926. Underneath the "locomotive" body is a Chevrolet one-ton truck chassis. Rather than riding on rails, the tug-and-trailer combination moved around on rubber tires, advertising the Chevrolet name as well as the circus. (N.)

This billboard proclaims Chevrolet's sales leadership in 1927 and shows a Chevrolet Capitol AA Series Sport Cabriolet. But everyone knew Chevrolet had gained it by default: Ford shut down its Model T assembly lines for six months at the end of May 1927 to retool for production of its new Model A. Chevrolet sales that year were 752,642, or 260,000 greater than Ford, whose dealer inventories were scant. After that year, Chevrolet rarely lost its lead. (G.)

William S. Knudsen, general manager of Chevrolet, was elected vice president of General Motors and a member of the GM Board of Directors on January 15, 1924, in recognition of his leadership, even before Chevrolet's sales triumph over his former employer, Ford. He is second from right in this undated portrait of a GM board meeting. (G.)

Another banner year for Chevrolet was 1928, when it outsold Ford by a large margin domestically and even internationally. In this photograph from GM of Brazil, "No. 1" on the left is a 1925 truck, the first Chevrolet assembled in Brazil. In only three years, Brazil made its 50,000th Chevrolet (right). (N.)

Two dapper salesmen wait for customers in a typical Chevrolet dealership showroom in 1928, with potted plants and a display of popular models: a roadster (left), a coach (center), and a touring car (far right). (N.)

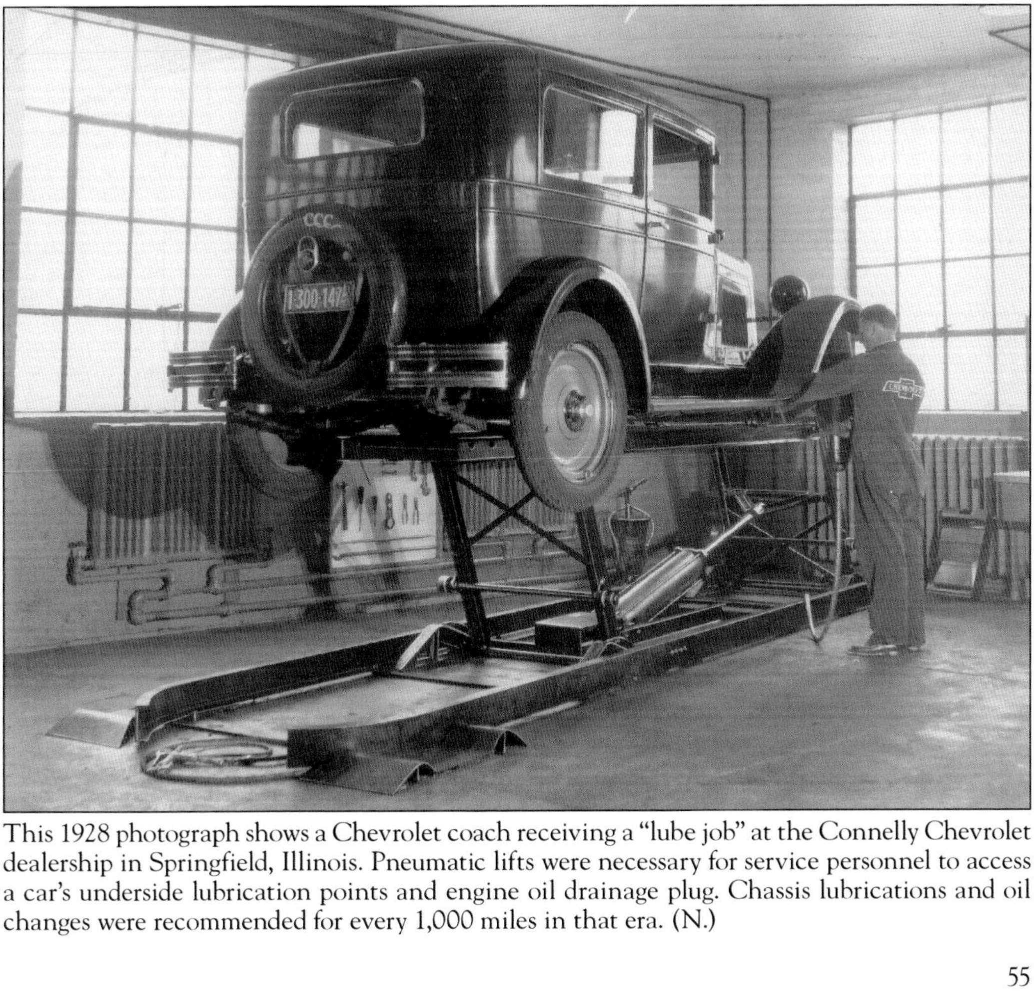

This 1928 photograph shows a Chevrolet coach receiving a "lube job" at the Connelly Chevrolet dealership in Springfield, Illinois. Pneumatic lifts were necessary for service personnel to access a car's underside lubrication points and engine oil drainage plug. Chassis lubrications and oil changes were recommended for every 1,000 miles in that era. (N.)

Chevrolet's four-millionth car, a $595 1928 National AB Series coach, was produced in Flint on January 11, 1928, just 363 days after the three-millionth. Chevrolet President and General Manager W.S. Knudsen stands on the right. As a step in the transition to a Six for the following year, the 1928 model had a longer 107-inch wheelbase and redesigned radiator shell. These alterations typified GM's new "annual model change" policy to boost sales. (N.)

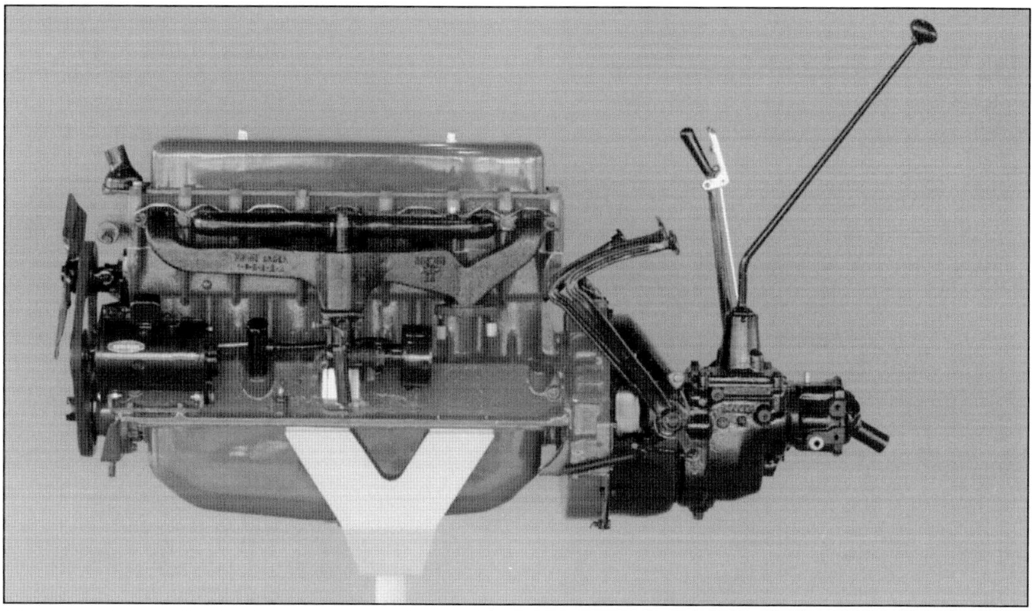

Chevrolet's six-cylinder "for the price of a four" engine was introduced for 1929 and assured Chevy's sales leadership for most of the ensuing decades. The 194-cid OHV Six produced 46 horsepower, with displacement and horsepower increasing in later years. The basic design exclusively powered Chevrolets until the 1955 models, when the small-block V8 became an option. The OHV Six continued to be offered until 1980, when it was replaced by a V6. (G.)

Perhaps to demonstrate the power of the new Six, Chevrolet publicists provided this photograph of a 1929 Chevrolet International Series AC coach ready to tow a sizeable trailer. The car's four-inch-longer 107-inch wheelbase provided for the longer engine. With its new Model A in place of the old Model T, Ford recovered sales leadership from Chevrolet in 1929 and 1930. (N.)

This top-of-the-line 1929 International Series AC Landau, a four-door sedan with a convertible roof over the rear seat, sold for $725, but relatively few—only 300—were built. The coach model was most popular, with 367,000 produced, followed by the four-door sedan (196,000), cabriolet (46,000), imperial sedan (42,000), and roadster (28,000). Only 8,600 phaeton models—the once popular open four-door Chevrolet, formerly known as a touring car—were built. (N.)

Historians debate whether this 1929 half-ton roadster was Chevrolet's first truck-based pickup or if the first "real" Chevrolet pickup truck came in 1934. In common with 1929 cars, this vehicle had the new OHV Six mounted on the longer wheelbase. Turn to page 51 to compare this truck-body-based pickup with the car-body model, both with soft tops. It appears this truck version has more cargo space and thus greater weight-carrying ability than the 1926 model. (N.)

Although new paved highways connecting cities became the norm in the 1920s, most roads in America were still dirt or gravel-surfaced at best. Accordingly, Chevrolet engineers devised this dust test to evaluate the effectiveness of a new carburetor air cleaner in conditions such as following another vehicle on a dusty road. The rear wheels are jacked up so that the engine can be run at any speed. (N.)

This fire engine is a 1930 Chevrolet. The new Six, along with a beefed-up chassis, allowed Chevrolet trucks to advance to the heavier 1.5-ton hauling class. In 1930, Chevrolet purchased the Martin Parry truck body company, which had been providing most truck bodies for Chevrolets. (N.)

This sport roadster was one of three new body types added to the Chevrolet line for 1930. The caption with the photograph proclaimed that the model "is destined to become a popular sight at the campuses and country clubs of the country"—the effects of the stock market crash only weeks earlier had not yet been noted. Wire wheels were a new option, replacing the steel disc wheels in use since 1924. (N.)

This aerial photograph from the 1930s shows the Chevrolet manufacturing complex on Flint's west side. In the left foreground is a Fisher Body plant, connected by a bridge over Chevrolet Avenue to carry newly fashioned vehicle bodies across to the car assembly plant. The Flint River runs past, with Chevrolet manufacturing plants on the right (south) side of the winding stream in this northwest view. The same area had been filled with sawmills and buggy factories 50 years earlier. (K.)

Chevrolet produced this roadster, its eight-millionth vehicle, in August 1931. Among other Chevrolet executives in the picture, Knudsen stands at the far left. The headline on the publicity photograph called the benchmark a "Depression Blues Chaser" because usual summer layoffs of production workers had been avoided. (N.)

In the 1930s, dealerships used three-wheeled motorcycles for service personnel to pick up and deliver customers' vehicles. This image also shows the evolution of car body designs with the rounding on the upper rear of the 1931 Chevrolet Independence Series AE coach. (N.)

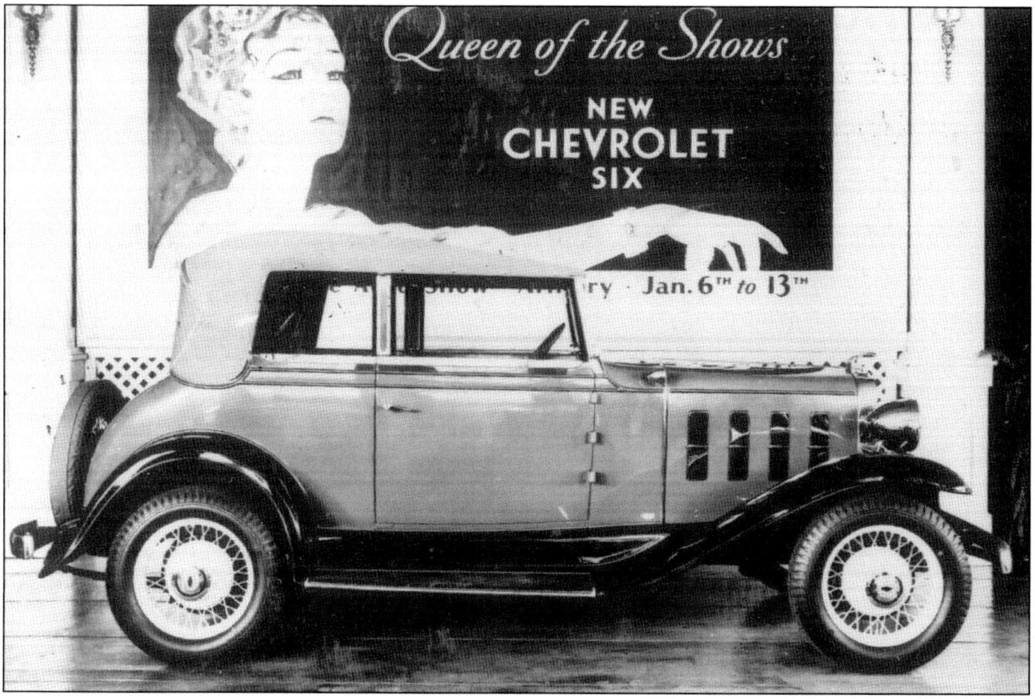

Parked in front of a billboard for an upcoming auto show is this snappy, top-of-the-line, 1932 Confederate Series BA Landau Phaeton. Increased compression ratio on the engine raised horsepower to 60 and wheel size was lowered to 18 inches. Distinctive louvers, or ventilator doors, on the hood sides mark it as a 1932 model. (G.)

Chevrolet design advanced in 1933 with this Master Eagle Series CA Deluxe Town Sedan model, featuring an enclosed trunk built into the body. Coach bodies had easily been Chevrolet's most popular body style since at least 1927, but the 1933 models came in two sizes: this upper series on a 110-inch wheelbase and a "Depression Chevy" Standard Series CC on a 107-inch chassis. (N.)

Four

The Depression Years 1934–1940

On October 16, 1933, the most important era in Chevrolet's history ended when William S. Knudsen (right) was elected executive vice president of General Motors in charge of all automotive operations. He was succeeded as president and general manager of Chevrolet by Marvin E. Coyle (left). Here they shake hands as the Chevrolet baton passes from Knudsen to Coyle. Coyle went on to be the longest-serving general manager in Chevrolet history, holding the post until after World War II. (G.)

This artist's rendering shows the mammoth Chevrolet exhibit at the General Motors building at the 1933 Chicago "A Century of Progress" World's Fair. Visitors could watch new Chevrolets being built from scratch and actually buy one there and drive it home. The left two production lines show Fisher bodies being welded and trimmed, and the right features Chevrolet Master Six coaches and coupes being assembled, to be driven off the line when completed. (N.)

The Chevrolet Soap Box Derby began in 1933 in Dayton, Ohio. The brainchild of newspaper photographer Myron Scott, it was a local newspaper event. Scott later moved to a sister newspaper in Akron, Ohio, and there sold sponsorship of the event—and himself—to Chevrolet. It became the largest spectator competition event in the country, and drew tens of thousands of potential customers to Chevrolet dealerships where entry registrations had to be made. (G.)

Chevrolet marketed two different car sizes for 1933: the upscale Master Eagle CA Series (page 62) and a new, smaller, economized $455 Standard Series CC "Depression Chevrolet," seen here in the coach body. The CC was offered only in two coupe versions and the coach version, with prices from $445 to $475. The upper series was full line with eight different bodies. (G.)

Here are the two sizes of 1933 Chevrolets, the Master Eagle CA with 110-inch wheelbase (left), and the Standard CC with a shorter 107-inch wheelbase (right). The differences are seen in careful comparison of the two photographs. The Eagle has a longer hood, chromed headlamps, a flute horn, hinged ventilator doors, and a hood ornament. (N.)

This phantom image of a 1933 Chevrolet sedan shows Fisher Body's extensive use of wood in framing the inner panels of the body and doors, a carryover from the buggy construction of the 19th century. But wooden parts rotted and squeaked, and the move to all-steel bodies was coming. Fisher was an independent body builder folded into GM in two actions between 1919 and 1927. By the early 1930s, all GM car assembly plants had Fisher Body plants attached and thus Fisher controlled the overall body design of all GM cars. (N.)

With the end of Prohibition in 1933, re-equipping the once-again legitimate liquor, wine, and beer industry was important business for vehicle makers, and Chevrolet produced this 1934 beer distributor truck. This photograph came from a body company mounting special bodies on the Chevrolet one-ton or 1.5-ton chassis. (N.)

This photograph illustrates the difference between the "three-window" (right) and the "five-window" (left) coupes of the 1930s, when those models were at the peak of their sales appeal. The "three-window" coupe (right) had only one side window on each side, whereas the "five" had two windows on each side (left). The back window was counted but the windshield was not. (N.)

The larger 1934 Chevrolet Master Series featured "Knee-Action" front suspension, promoted in this billboard poster. Other improvements for the Master were a new "YK" frame and revised cylinder head and rocker arm designs for the enlarged "Blue Flame" OHV Six, now producing 80 horsepower from 207-cid to compete with Ford's 85-horsepower V8 and the 77-horsepower Plymouth L-head Six. The Standard Series for 1934 was mostly a carryover from 1933 models. (G.)

Chevrolet's 10-millionth car, a 1934 Standard four-door sedan built on November 13, 1934, was presented to the city of Flint's police department for use in "Safety Patrol Work." Chevrolet continued to offer two series in two sizes of 1934 models. Master Series production of 457,000 was nearly five times that of the Standard Series. (G.)

These chassis line workers at the Chevrolet Flint assembly plant mount the grille for a 1935 Chevrolet as the frames move along from left to right. The engine-transmission unit and radiator have not yet been installed; it was likely the next step in the assembly process, followed by fastening fenders and then the important "drop" onto the frame of a fully trimmed Fisher Body from an adjoining plant. (G)

This final inspection line at the Chevrolet plant was where new cars were checked after final assembly before being driven to a storage yard for transfer to railroad cars or haul-away trucks for shipment to dealers and customers. In the adjoining area at the left, vehicles, including a dual-rear-wheel truck also made in the plant, awaited adjustments before being shipped out. (G.)

Here are two different series—and sizes—of Chevrolet cars for 1935. Above is a low-end $550 Standard EC Series four-door model, largely a carryover in design and noticeably shorter, with a 107-inch wheelbase, than the upscale $580 Master Deluxe Series two-door coach model (below) mounted on a 113-inch wheelbase. The upscale 1935 had a new split windshield and both series were now equipped with the 207-cid OHV Six. The high-end series featured Fisher Body's new all-steel "Turret Top," seen below. (N.)

This 1935 Chevrolet Sedan Delivery commercial vehicle was rated as a truck but was built on the passenger car chassis with the 1934 Standard Series passenger car front-end appearance. Note the spare tire on the side "fender mount" because the vehicle's cargo area and side-hinged rear door left no place for a spare. This year Ford managed to gain the sales crown over Chevrolet, 826,500 to 657,000, because Chevrolet encountered production constraints. (N.)

The Chevrolet Suburban "Carry-All" eight-passenger vehicle, shown here, was introduced mid-year 1935 on the half-ton truck chassis with a light truck appearance. The first Suburban had a 112-inch wheelbase—an inch less than the Master Deluxe Series car—and the same size engine, but derated with a lower compression ratio and a slower turning speed to 60 horsepower. (G.)

Realizing it had to keep up with the pace of vehicle advances since 1918, the US Army ordered 250 Chevrolet 1.5-ton two-axle trucks from the Oakland, California, assembly plant. This truck type, on a 131-inch wheelbase, was later produced in large numbers during World War II for the War Department (page 94). Here, several dozen have been unloaded from haul-away trucks for delivery at an unidentified western US Army post. (N.)

The same 1.5-ton Chevrolet truck chassis as above demonstrates hauling a 13,000-pound tracked vehicle on a flatbed trailer. Specialist truck companies like Mack, White, Reo, and International manufactured most heavy-duty trucks at the time. After World War II, the Detroit carmakers began producing and marketing heavy trucks, but largely withdrew from that market toward the end of the 20th century. (N.)

Here are two different versions of what were labeled 1936 Chevrolet light trucks. Above is a pickup truck based on the 1934–1935 light truck design. Below is a "1936 ½" sedan delivery with the upper series 1935 Master Deluxe passenger-car all-steel "Turret Top" and two-piece windshield. Chevrolet marketed at least three different types of light commercial vehicles for 1936: two on different-length car chassis and one on the half-ton truck frame. Their detailed specifications and volumes are sparse today. (N.)

The 1936 Chevrolet passenger cars again presented "new model year" appearance changes but continued in two different sizes and series. At the top is a stylish "three-window" Master Deluxe Series coupe with a rumble seat and optional streamlining "wheel pants" covering the rear wheel openings. Below is an unusual "five-window" Coupe Pickup model with the spare in the front fender, similar in concept to the 1926 roadster pickup (page 51). The number of available open models—roadsters, convertibles/cabriolets, and phaetons—was reduced from four in 1935 to just a single convertible model for 1936, signifying the big change in car buyers' tastes since the mid-1920s. Chevrolet bounced back from its prior-year sales loss to Ford, selling 930,000 to Ford's 749,000. (N.)

The all-steel top was a major focus of Chevrolet promotion for its 1936 models. This photograph shows the major part of a November 1935 New York auto show exhibit devoted to Fisher Body and its steel stampings. The large one-piece stampings making the Turret Top possible involved both the development of large stamping presses and advanced metallurgy to make the pressed steel stretch and bend without cracking. (N.)

Here is a display of Chevrolet commercial vehicles at what was labeled the "1936 NY Truck Show." It is not known whether "1936" referred to the model year of the trucks or to the calendar year of the event. Sales personnel and potential customers mingled around the exhibits. On the left, a 1935–1936 Chevrolet pickup truck was displayed beside the panel truck in the center background. (N.)

Some automobile dealers were able to invest in large-scale shows to attract customers to new models, like the A.J. Morrison Chevrolet dealer show of 1936 models in Sacramento, California. The show, displaying the complete array of Chevrolet's cars, of which there were a dozen different versions—coupes, coaches, sedans, and the single cabriolet convertible—continued for eight days. Truck models were located at the rear. (N.)

Chevrolet had two series for 1937 models, the Master and the Master Deluxe, both in the same size and styling on 112-inch wheelbases and with a newly enlarged and more powerful 216.5-cid, 85-horsepower engine. Here is the front view of a 1937 sedan. There were 12 different models between the two series, with prices ranging from $619 for a Master coupe to $788 for a Master Deluxe sport sedan. (N.)

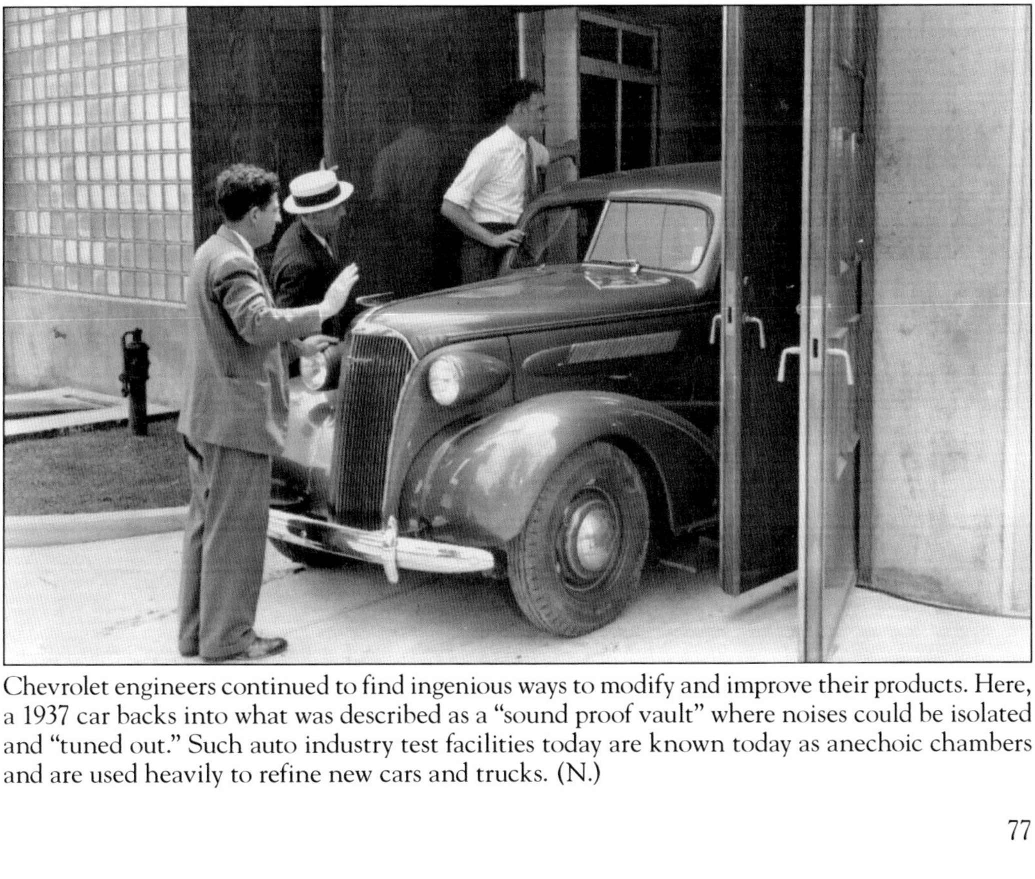

Chevrolet engineers continued to find ingenious ways to modify and improve their products. Here, a 1937 car backs into what was described as a "sound proof vault" where noises could be isolated and "tuned out." Such auto industry test facilities today are known today as anechoic chambers and are used heavily to refine new cars and trucks. (N.)

Chevrolet heavy trucks for 1937 used frontal styling similar to passenger cars of the same model year. This 1.5-ton truck with an unusual open cab holds several cows in a homemade cattle pen on the back. It appears to be a genuine working truck scene and not something artificially staged by professional photographers working from Detroit studios. (N.)

The Chevrolet "step-van" for stop-and-start local service such as laundry/dry cleaning or milk delivery was a new concept in truck bodies. This vehicle, for "step-in delivery," initially called Dubl-Duty, was based on a half-ton truck chassis. In 1937, the Chevrolet-Ford sales contest was extremely close; Chevrolet had 768,000 new car and truck registrations and Ford had 765,900. (N.)

All large-scale American factory production was disrupted in 1937–1938 by union-organized strikes for bargaining recognition at steel, rubber, and auto plants. The United Auto Workers (UAW) virtually shut down GM with sit-down strikes in Cleveland and at Flint's Fisher Body plants 1 and 2, beginning just before the end of 1937. This photograph shows strikers passing time inside Fisher No. 1, the supplier of bodies to Flint's Buick assembly plants and metal stampings for several other GM plants. (D.)

The Flint strike grew ugly early in 1938 when crowds massed in support of workers inside the plants. Widespread damage and injury was feared and Michigan's governor called in National Guard troops to prevent violence and protect property. Here, the troops unload from 1935 Chevrolet army trucks (see page 72) and muster outside Fisher No. 2 on Chevrolet Avenue. General Motors capitulated after 44 days and signed its first contract with the UAW. (D.)

This Chevrolet dealership in St. Petersburg, Florida, was typical of prewar US auto stores. GM had a peak of 17,360 domestic dealers in 1941 with average dealer sales of 107 new vehicles yearly and 190,000 total employees. After World War II, the trend was to fewer but larger dealerships. Dealer sales averaged 222 new units in the boom year of 1955 and nearly 300 per year in the early 1960s, when GM's US dealership employment reached 275,000. (N.)

The 1938 Chevrolet shown here, a right-hand-drive model, was the 100,000th Chevrolet assembled by GM in South Africa. Chevrolet had a large export operation in New Jersey to box incompletely assembled vehicles, which were then shipped overseas for final assembly with varying amounts of local content such as glass, upholstery, tires, and sometimes entire bodies. (G.)

This 1938 Chevrolet sedan was used as a mobile demonstration vehicle for the Pan-Am Oil Company—the rear door labeling reads "Pan-Am Talking Automobile." The hood has been modified to open in one piece and an oilcan is displayed atop the engine. Such promotional arrangements benefited both Chevrolet and the oil company. Car sales for the industry were down sharply in 1938, from nearly 3.5 million in 1937 to 1.9 million. (N.)

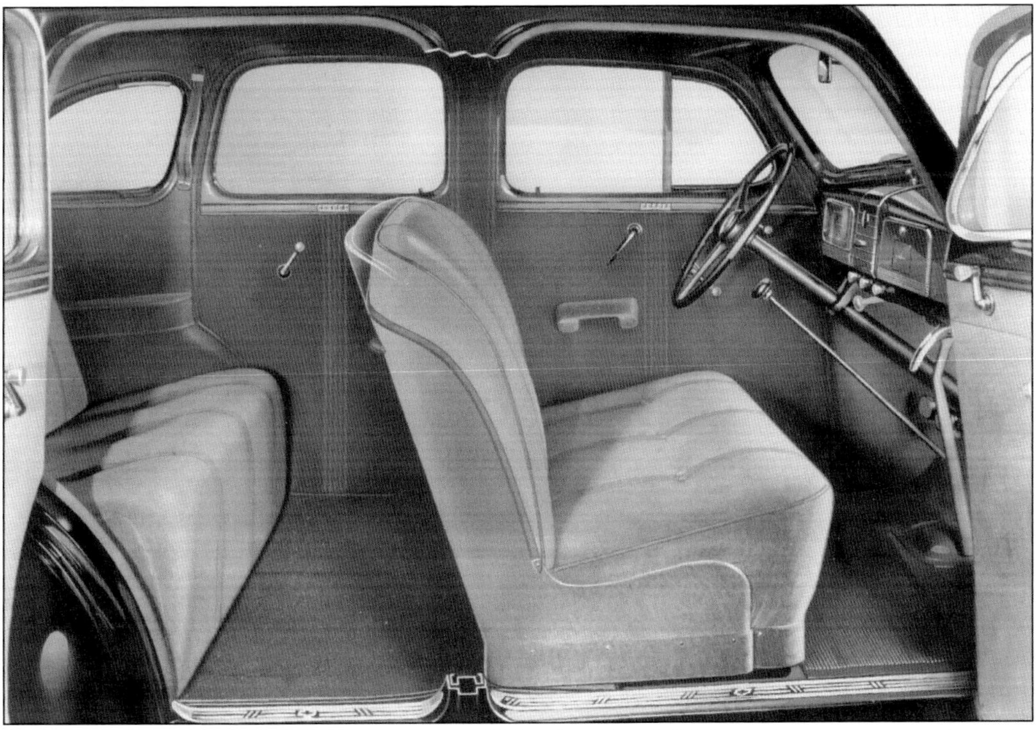

This studio photograph shows the center, or "B," pillar of a 1938 Chevrolet cut away to show the spaciousness of the four-door sedan. Note that the transmission control is still mounted on the floor, though placed forward to allow foot room for a center-front passenger. Rear compartment space was huge compared to modern cars. (N.)

Despite the roominess of the standard 1938 Chevrolet sedan on the previous page, this catalogue illustration shows a "stretch" body version designated for taxi service. Note the taxi light on the front of the roof. Such long-bodied Chevrolets could be manufactured in the same Fisher Body plant in Detroit that made Cadillac limousines. (N.)

This 1938 Chevrolet 1.5-ton dump truck hauls a load of sand or dirt out of a ditch. Continuing the practice adopted in 1937, the truck front-end appearance is nearly identical to 1938 Chevrolet passenger cars. The truck would have been supplied in cab-and-chassis form to a company building and installing universal dump truck bodies and lifting mechanisms. (N.)

This auto show display introducing the 1939 Chevrolet makes a value comparison between a $647 1928 Chevrolet coach and the $646 1939. It listed more than 22 improvements and was a larger car with a more powerful engine—85 horsepower versus 35. Evidently, few bothered to check the boastful figures because the *Standard Catalogue* lists the 1928 price as $585 and the 1939 as $648. (N.)

Chevrolet introduced an entirely new factory-supplied body type for 1939. The "woody" station wagon was offered in two series, Master 85 for $848 and Master Deluxe for $883. They were the highest-priced Chevrolets that year. About 1,400 1939 station wagons were produced out of 587,000 Chevrolets total. The largest-selling Chevy body style remained the two-door sedan, or coach, selling about 357,000 total units. (N.)

Chevrolet offered no roadster, phaeton, cabriolet, or convertible model for 1939. It was the only peacetime year when no fresh-air US Chevys were available in the brand's first 65 years. Here, however, is an artist's rendering, perhaps from the GM Styling department, of what a 1939 Chevy convertible might have looked like. (N.)

GM Overseas negotiated a sale to the Swiss Army of the 15 1939 Chevrolet convertible four-door sedans shown here. The phaeton or touring car bodies were probably custom-made at a European body company. Any of these cars remaining in existence would be among the rarest and most collectible Chevys ever produced. (G.)

This photograph of a 1939 Chevy Sedan Delivery used by the Port Huron, Michigan, *Times Herald* for newspaper delivery illustrates the fact that up until the 1960s, virtually all American cars were front-engine/rear-drive and managed to maneuver through snow-covered roads regularly with little complaint. During the 1930s, the slang expression "Chevy" came into wide and endearing use among Chevrolet enthusiasts, although some recall the name being used as early as 1920. In Canada, it was merely "Chev," and in the South, it was pronounced "Shivvy." (N.)

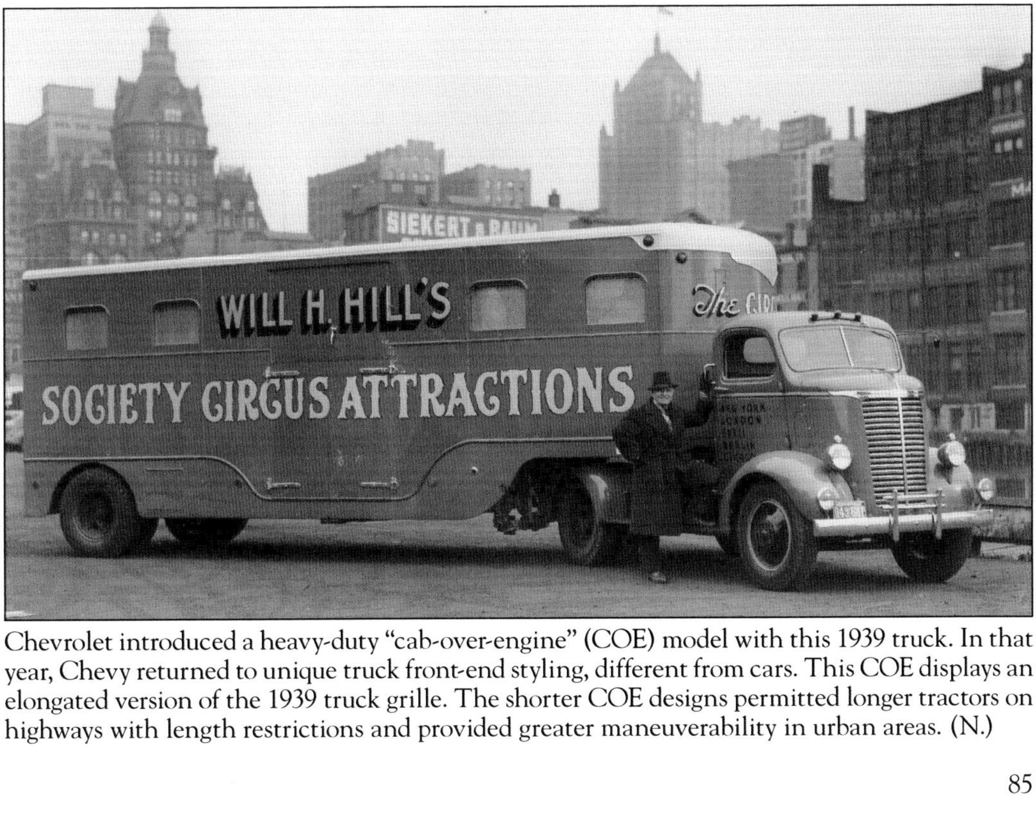

Chevrolet introduced a heavy-duty "cab-over-engine" (COE) model with this 1939 truck. In that year, Chevy returned to unique truck front-end styling, different from cars. This COE displays an elongated version of the 1939 truck grille. The shorter COE designs permitted longer tractors on highways with length restrictions and provided greater maneuverability in urban areas. (N.)

World War II had broken out in Europe in 1939 and would soon affect the US automotive industry with diminution of export sales, material shortages, and the need for different products. Typical of the different products is this special heavy-duty, 1.5-ton 1940 Chevrolet panel truck provided to the Red Cross for children's refugee relief. Note the dual rear wheels to provide extra load capacity and the carryover truck grille from 1939. (N.)

With the 1940 model year, Chevrolet once again offered a "rag-top," or convertible body, as shown here in this catalogue illustration. Factory-priced at $898, this four-passenger Special Deluxe model was the most expensive Chevrolet except for two station wagon models. The Chevys of 1940 were offered in three series: Master 85 KB, Master Deluxe KH, and Special Deluxe KA, with 14 different models, all featuring the standard 216.5-cid OHV Six on a 113-inch wheelbase. (N.)

At the opposite end of the Chevrolet model spectrum for 1940 was this $659 two-person Master 85 Series Business Coupe, shown here in Bell Telephone Company service on a Michigan residential street. New registrations of Chevrolet cars and trucks reached nearly 854,000 in 1940, far ahead of Ford's 543,000. (N.)

This view of the celebration of GM's 25-millionth car production is slightly different from that on this volume's cover. GM President William S. Knudsen is at the microphone, with Chevrolet General Manager Marvin E. Coyle on his right and GM Chairman Alfred P. Sloan Jr. and GM Executive Vice President Charles E. Wilson to his left. GM graciously invited founder William C. Durant, long absent from GM ranks, to its January 11, 1940, celebration banquet at Detroit's Masonic Auditorium. (N.)

Five

WORLD WAR II AND POSTWAR 1941–1952

For the auto industry and Chevrolet, World War II started 18 months before the December 1941 Japanese attack on Pearl Harbor. In late May 1940, after the Nazi blitzkrieg swept across Belgium and France, Pres. Franklin D. Roosevelt asked GM president and Chevrolet builder William S. Knudsen to resign his corporate position and become, in effect, the czar of American defense production. This advertisement matches Chevrolet's World War II military and prewar civilian trucks. (G.)

Meanwhile, the civilian vehicle business continued for automakers. In the spring of 1941, Chevrolet introduced a new body type, the upper series Special Deluxe Fleetline, featuring a "torpedo body" four-door sedan with two side windows (above). At $877, the Fleetline was Chevy's third most expensive car. The conventional 1941 lower series Chevrolet Master Deluxe Sport Sedan is shown below with three side windows. The bodies for all 1941 Chevrolet cars rode on a three-inch longer 116-inch wheelbase. The 216.5-cid OHV Six had a higher compression ratio, giving it 90 horsepower. (N.)

Despite the war clouds of 1940–1941, Americans still used their cars for recreational opportunities. This couple gets ready to go fishing in their $851 1941 Chevrolet Special Deluxe Sport Sedan. Note the two-tone paint application, an extra cost option that became popular for GM products and was also offered by Chrysler, and—with very limited popularity—by Ford. Chevrolet's 1941 new vehicle registrations totaled 1.3 million, versus strike-struck Ford's 748,000. (N.)

Chevrolet trucks again took on front styling distinct from 1941 Chevy passenger cars, as shown here on this COE model. The headlamp pods partially in the fenders resemble those of 1940 model Chevrolet cars. Light trucks constituted only 11 percent of total vehicle sales in 1941, in contrast to the first decade of the 21st century when, augmented by vans and SUVs, they came to more than 50 percent. (N.)

Continuing as the most popular Chevrolet body in 1941 was this two-door style. Listed as the Town Sedan by its maker, most owners called the style a coach or referred to it merely as a two-door sedan. Town Sedan production of the two 1941 series combined came to 448,000. Starting that same year, external running boards no longer appeared on Chevrolet cars. (N.)

For its 1942 models introduced in September 1941 and planned two to three years earlier, Chevrolet unveiled this racy Fleetline Series two-door sedan named Aerosedan, a style that came to be known as "fastback" in contrast to the "flatback," "trunkback" or "notchback" designs of conventional Chevrolet sedans. After World War II, Chevrolet continued to produce fastback designs through 1952. (N.)

As the sign on this 1942 Chevrolet proclaims, "Last Chevrolet Until The War Is Won," this was Chevy's last passenger vehicle produced as plants switched to war production. Assembly was completed on January 30, 1942, barely seven weeks after the Pearl Harbor attack. Only 258,795 1942 Chevy cars had been built. (G.)

This wartime advertisement proclaims that Chevrolet was building everything "from Ducks to Trucks" for the war effort. Chevrolet war production contributions are illustrated with photographs or artwork of aircraft—for which Chevrolet built engines—aircraft engine propeller blades, anti-aircraft guns, artillery shells, trucks, and sister GMC Division's famous amphibious DUKW "Duck" trucks. (G.)

This is the government issue version of Chevrolet's 1.5-ton truck, equipped with four-wheel drive and modified to Army specifications for carrying both men and material. It was smaller than GMC Division's 6-by-6 2.5-ton Army truck. The wartime advertisement on page 89 shows how the military and civilian versions of Chevy's 1.5-ton differed. (D.)

This unique M38 Wolfhound six-wheeled armored car, powered by a Cadillac V8 with Hydra-Matic transmission, was developed by Chevrolet for the Army late in World War II. Weighing 15,300 pounds and mounting a four-man crew, the M38 was designed to replace the M8 armored car. Armament consisted of a 37-mm cannon plus single 50-caliber and 30-caliber machine guns. Approved in March 1945, it was unlikely to have seen much, if any, combat. (D.)

This is a formal portrait of Lt. Gen. William S. Knudsen, the first civilian commissioned as a general, an honor bestowed on him by Roosevelt in February 1942 for mobilizing US industry for defense and then war production. Knudsen was a Danish immigrant who rose from the shop floor to become general manager of Chevrolet and later president of General Motors. He was Detroit's, GM's, and Chevrolet's, greatest contribution to winning the war. (G.)

Nicholas Dreystadt had been a GM vice president and general manager of Cadillac for 12 years when the corporation selected him to succeed Marvin E. Coyle at Chevrolet on June 13, 1946, to guide the Division's postwar recovery back to full production. His efforts were cut short, however, when he died of cancer on September 3, 1948, just three months before the introduction of the sleek new 1949 Chevrolets. (G.)

The first postwar Chevrolet passenger car comes off the line at a Chevrolet assembly plant on October 3, 1945, greeted by two Chevrolet officials. Unfortunately, output to fill pent-up demand after more than three years of war production was long delayed. On November 21, 1945, the UAW began a 113-day strike against GM, seeking to bargain on vehicle prices but eventually settling for a wage increase. (G.)

This is a catalogue illustration of a Chevrolet vehicle evidently unknown in the United States. It appears to be a "woody" station wagon body mounted on a half-ton 1946 truck chassis. The license plate indicates a foreign country. The demand for new cars and trucks was even more severe overseas than in America because vehicles and production facilities had been destroyed or damaged in World War II. (N.)

This publicity photograph celebrates both the new postwar Chevy and the 50th anniversary in 1946 of the US post office rural free delivery (RFD) system. The caption on the print stated that the woman was giving her mailman homemade doughnuts to honor his service. "Approximately 26 million Americans are served by RFD, and with U.S. Mail traveling by skis, dog-sleds, ice-boats and snowshoes, Carrier Dolph gets there faster in his new Chevrolet," the caption said. (N.)

This high-angle view of a 1947 Chevrolet two-door sedan shows the modest "facelift" styling changes made between the 1946 and 1947 models. The bright metal molding below the belt line of the 1946, stretching from near the front of the hood to near the car's rear, was replaced in 1947 by a short spear on the hood side, and the rounded chrome molding around the grille was removed. (N.)

This 1947 Chevrolet Panel Delivery model was converted for use as a funeral home or mortuary remains-transportation vehicle. It was essentially a carryover from 1942 prewar Chevy cars, and sedan deliveries were built on a 116-inch wheelbase chassis powered by the "Cast-Iron Wonder"—also known as "Stovebolt"—OHV Six engine and three-speed manual synchromesh transmission, with the shift lever mounted on the steering column. (N.)

Production commenced on May 1, 1947, for the postwar 1948 Chevrolet light trucks with a new cab and front-end design shown in this catalogue illustration. They were offered in half-ton EP Series 3100, three-quarter-ton ER Series 3600, and one-ton ES Series 3800 configurations with corresponding wheelbases of 116, 125, and 137 inches, and branded as "Thriftmaster." (N.)

The rear quarter view of a lower series 1947 Chevrolet Stylemaster Sport Sedan shows the typical modest trim and tiny tail lamps of prewar and postwar cars. This body was basically a carryover from the 1942 models. The postwar auto industry faced both disruptive labor situations and acute material shortages. Many early models were shipped with wooden beams as bumpers, to be exchanged when chromed steel replacements became available. (N.)

The front end of a 1948 Chevrolet again shows very little change from 1947 models. To maintain the pattern of annual model change, a T-shaped vertical bar was mounted in the center of the grille and a new hood ornament and emblem were added, which were subtle changes at best as the division prepared to bring out 1949 models with totally different bodies. In the postwar period, four-door sedans displaced two-door sedans as the most popular body style. (N.)

This 1948 Fleetmaster Convertible Coupe was Chevrolet's first "pace car" at the Indianapolis 500 Memorial Day Race. It was the first of 22 Chevrolets to pace the track over the next 63 years. The 1948 and a 1955 Bel Air convertible pace cars were the only "standard" Chevrolets; the rest have been Corvettes (10), Camaros (7), a Beretta, a Monte Carlo, and an SSR. With its trusty six-cylinder engine, the Fleetmaster was hardly a racecar, but it could probably maintain 85–90 miles per hour without tweaking. (G.)

Passenger car interiors of the 1940s were quite spacious, even if they were probably exaggerated for this 1948 Chevrolet catalogue. Car bodies were positioned atop the frame, the result being that the driveshaft tunnel hardly protruded into the rear floor. Interior trim would have been natural fabrics with rubber floor mats in front and floor carpeting behind the front seat. The image shows why they were called bench seats. (N.)

This catalogue illustration of a 1948 Fleetmaster station wagon is distorted, as was the custom, to make the car look longer. This model was the last year of pure "woodies" for Chevrolet. Such vehicles were becoming fashionable for the upwardly mobile and were practical for groups needing to carry more than six persons. With its third-row, leather-covered bench seat, the 1948 Chevy wagon could carry eight occupants. (N.)

The 1949 Chevrolet Styleline Deluxe Series eight-passenger station wagon featured an all-new streamlined body. The early 1949 station wagon body was no longer made entirely of wood, and during the model year, Chevrolet phased in an all-steel version of the design fitted with faux wood appliqués. This image also illustrates the new curved windshield glass for 1949. (N.)

Above is the 1949 Fleetline four-door sedan with the new "fastback" roofline previously limited to Fleetline two-door sedans. It is posed with a US Air Force F-80 Shooting Star jet fighter, the symbol of speed and technology at the time. Below is the 1949 Styleline four-door with its "notch-back" body design adapted from the 1941 Fleetline four-door. Both sedans were factory-priced at $1,539, with carryover mechanicals from prior models and an inch shorter 115-inch wheelbase. (N.)

Chevrolet introduced two major innovations in the low-price field for 1950. First was the Bel Air two-door "hardtop" coupe shown here as a $1,741 Styleline Deluxe with extra-cost optional wide white sidewall tires and standard rear fender skirts. The Bel Air was premium-priced, more than the $1,498 Sport Coupe two-door with conventional roof, but less than the $1,847 convertible. (N.)

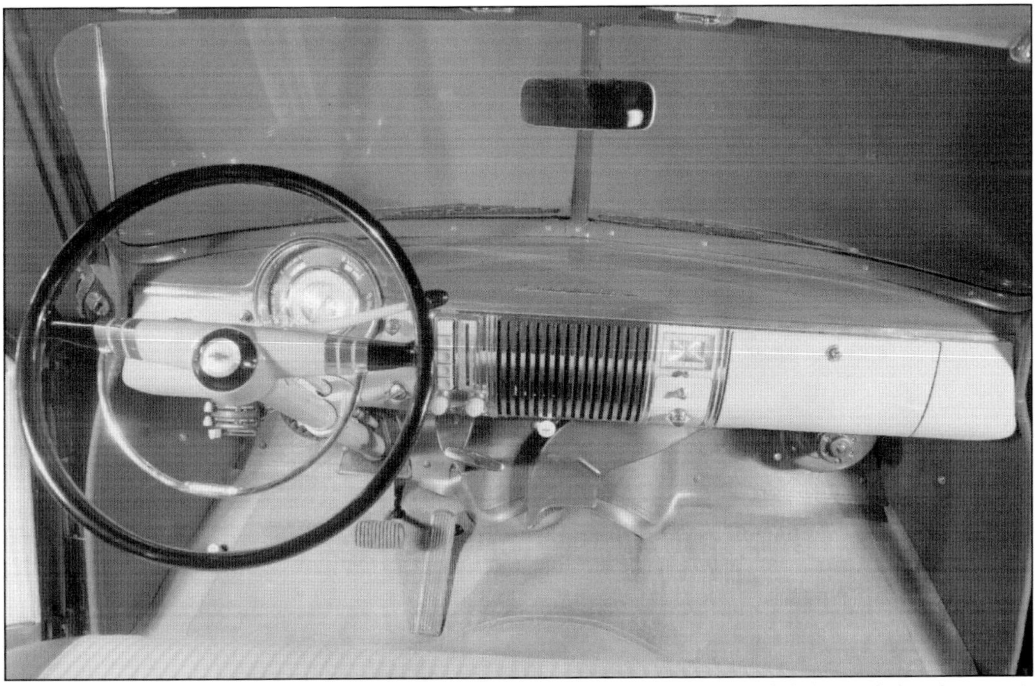

The second important Chevrolet innovation for 1950 was the availability of the division's own Powerglide torque-converter automatic transmission, the first automatic in the low-price field. The two-speed automatic was priced at $159 and was available only in the Deluxe Series. Absence of a clutch pedal left of the brake pedal is seen in this image of a Powerglide-equipped 1950 Chevrolet interior. (N.)

This 1949 Chevrolet 3100 half-ton truck with a canopy express body was a direct descendent of the first Chevrolet truck in 1918 (page 38). It shared the passenger car power train and was mounted on a 116-inch wheelbase. The heavier-duty Model 3800 one-ton Chevrolet truck had a floor-mounted, four-speed manual transmission. (N.)

Chevrolet continued to offer the sedan delivery body for light duty service. The 1951 model, seen in this catalogue illustration, was a model of the lower-series Styleline Special with black-wall tires and no rear fender skirts. Such vehicles were popular for customer distribution of bakery goods, groceries, laundry and dry cleaning, flowers, and the like. (N.)

This studio photograph of a Chevrolet Fleetline fastback two-door sedan illustrates the new styling modifications for the 1951 model. The caption pointed out that the grille and rear fenders were different from the 1950 model. The Korean War had broken out in mid-1950 and while Detroit's involvement was far less than in World War II, rising costs, material shortages, and diverted production still challenged Chevrolet and its competitors. (N.)

Fleet sales of new cars have always been a mainstay of the high-volume, low end of the market auto producers. Here is a field of hundreds of identical black 1951 Chevrolet Styleline sedans awaiting assignment to the fleet purchaser. With a $1,629 list price for the two-door sedan, these were the lowest priced Chevrolets offered, but a large fleet purchase would have earned considerably lower prices. (N.)

At a time when war-inflated prices were rapidly rising, this Chevrolet dealer in Spring Grove, Pennsylvania, displayed a new 1952 Chevrolet alongside a 1932 model with a signboard claiming the 1952 required only 23 weeks working at average wages to purchase, versus 37 weeks in 1932. Since the introduction of the six-cylinder engine in 1929, Chevrolet marketing had always emphasized the value aspect of buying Chevrolets. (N.)

This $2,191 1952 Chevrolet Styleline Deluxe station wagon was posed in a hunting environment, continuing the outdoorsy promotional theme shown with the 1941 model (page 91). The cargo capacity of the station wagon, especially with its third-row seat removed (which wasn't easy in those days), made it more practical than a mere sedan for carrying recreational gear. (N.)

Six

Competition and Corvettes 1953–1960

Chevrolet's business in the 1950s was marked by high-energy competition with other brands and on the racetrack. Here, Division General Manager Thomas H. Keating, who assumed the post on July 1, 1949, poses symbolically with a "winner" flag beside the 1955 Chevrolet Indy Pace Car powered by Chevy's new small-block V8. Chevrolet kept the competition active in the 1950s by pioneering new products and features for the low-priced field.

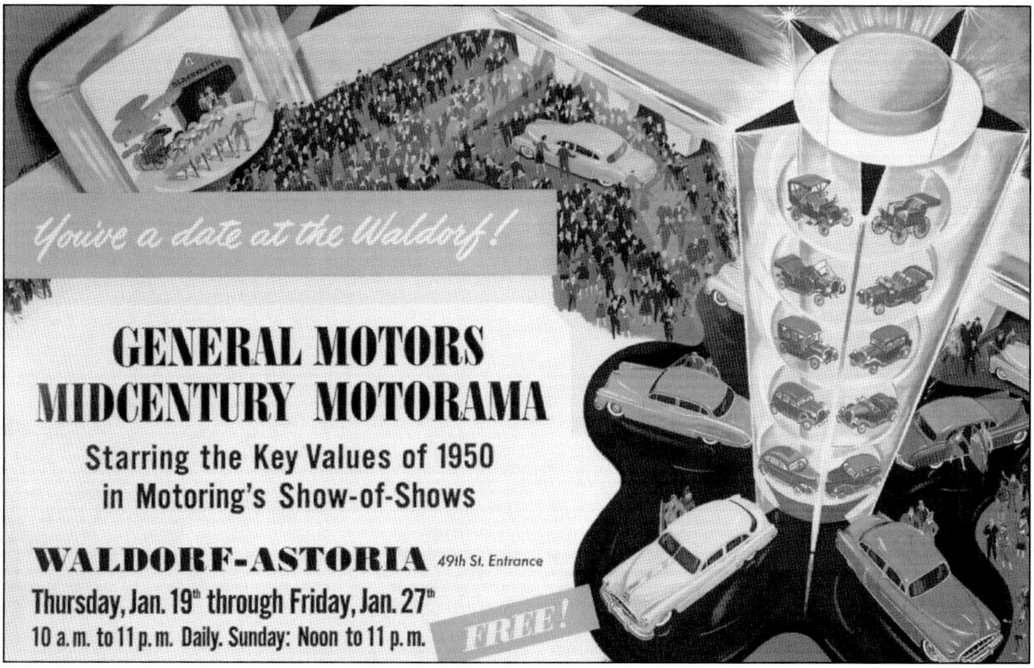

As the postwar auto business changed from a sellers' market to a buyers' market, GM stimulated public interest with its spectacular Motorama shows of the corporation's vehicles. This is an invitation to the 1950 event in New York City. Motoramas traveled across America, showcasing GM's "dream," or concept, cars to whet the buying public's appetite. (G.)

At the January 1953 Motorama premiere in New York City's Waldorf-Astoria Hotel, Chevrolet unveiled this two-seat Corvette sports car with a fiberglass rather than steel body. It created a sensation and Chevrolet moved speedily to put it into limited production to satisfy the implied public demand. The production car, seen on the next page, looked almost—but not quite—identical to the show car. (G.)

The first hand-built production Corvettes come off the line at Flint's Chevrolet Assembly plant on June 30, 1953, six months after the dream car unveiling in New York. All white with red vinyl interiors, they featured the newly enlarged 1953 Chevrolet 235.5-cid OHV Six, boosted to 150 horsepower with troublesome triple carburetors. The standard Powerglide automatic transmission appropriately had the shift lever floor-mounted. (G.)

General Motors initially seemed to treat the $3,498 Corvette as a separate brand from Chevrolet. This photograph, at GM's Mesa, Arizona, Desert Proving Ground, shows a Corvette leading a parade of other 1953 GM sedans—Buick, Chevrolet, Pontiac, Oldsmobile, and Cadillac. Corvette's glass fiber body was rustproof but also inhibited typical high volume automotive production; only 300 were built in 1953. (N.)

The big 1953 model news for most Chevrolet customers was the introduction of power steering, another first in the low-priced field. This publicity image shows how added power steering mechanical components fit into the engine compartment. The optional price for power steering was $178, the same as for the automatic transmission. The factory car prices in 1953 ranged from $1,524 for a 150 Series Business Coupe to $2,273 for a 210 Series eight-passenger station wagon. (G.)

The 1954 model year brought a revised front end appearance for Chevrolet light trucks, shown here on this Suburban. A new grille was mounted on the older truck cab design first introduced in 1947. In those years, the Suburban was mainly a work vehicle rather than a family or recreational hauler. Chevy trucks benefited from the larger 235.5-cid OHV Six engine introduced for 1953 cars and trucks. (N.)

1954 was the first year that popular entertainer Dinah Shore sang the memorable "See the USA in your Chevrolet" advertising theme song on her radio and TV shows, which were sponsored by Chevrolet through 1961. This photograph catches her enjoying one of the Chevrolet dream cars, probably at the 1954 Motorama show. In the memories of many in the older generation, Dinah, her theme song, and Chevrolet are inseparable. (G.)

Chevrolet cars for 1954 provided only minor changes from 1953, which in contrast had enjoyed substantial sheet metal differences from 1952. Here, a 210 Series Sedan and a 150 Series Station Wagon are seen outside the new ranch house design popular at the time. Growing families were moving to new homes in the suburbs and buying new cars for commuting and pleasure. Blue, red, and black colors became available for the Corvette and production moved from Flint to St. Louis. (G.)

The big Chevrolet news for 1955 was this 265-cid small-block OHV V8 engine, Chevy's first Eight since 1918. The 162-horsepower V8, along with the companion Corvette, dramatically changed Chevrolet's image from the value-oriented but stodgy family car, to a fashion statement and prospective performance king. (G.)

The signature model for Chevrolet in 1955 was this $2,166 Bel Air V8 hardtop. Bel Air had advanced from just a body-style model to Chevrolet's third series, with six all-new-design body choices—four-door sedan, two-door sedan, two-door hardtop (shown), convertible, two-door Nomad wagon, and four-door six-passenger station wagon. Two-tone, bright-color paint schemes on upper series reached down the car sides. Chevrolet won the 1955 sales battle with 1,970,472 new registrations to Ford's 1,869,176. (N.)

This is a rear view of the unusual 1955 Chevrolet Nomad station wagon which, like the Corvette, was originally shown as a dream car at a GM Motorama. It was designed to appeal to fashion-oriented buyers who still wanted to carry people and cargo like other wagons. At $2,571 when V8 equipped, it was the highest priced Chevy in 1955. (N.)

The 1955 model year completed the changeover to high-performance OHV V8 engines for all major Detroit automakers. It began with Cadillac and Olds (1949), Chrysler and Studebaker (1951), DeSoto and Lincoln (1952), Buick and Dodge (1953), and Ford and Mercury (1954). Joining Chevy for 1955 were Hudson, Nash, Packard, Plymouth, and Pontiac. Stockcar racing was still "showroom stock" at the time and most automakers competed on the tracks. Here, a newly competitive 1955 Chevy wins the Darlington 500 in South Carolina. (G.)

The instrument panel design theme of the limited-production 1953 Corvette sports roadster (above) strongly influenced that of conventional 1955 Chevrolet family sedans such as the one below. For 1955, Corvette had as standard Chevrolet's new V8 plus a manual transmission. It continued on its 102-inch wheelbase but the factory price of $2,934 had been reduced from the $3,523 price of the 1954 models. (N.)

General Motors produced its 50-millionth car in 1955, and a Flint-built Chevrolet Bel Air two-door hardtop was designated as the symbolic unit. This parade up Flint's main street celebrated the event before tens of thousands of spectators. It could be said that Flint was both Chevrolet's home and heart. (G.)

General Motors' great success in 1955 was augmented by introduction in the spring of an all-new truck cab, shown here in the upscale $3,355 Cameo pickup version, with box sides of fiberglass flush with the cab. The wraparound windshield and back window provided exceptional vision and the new 265-cid V8 was available. (N.)

In 1955, a total of 27 new 1955 Corvette roadsters took over the wrong side of a not-yet-opened Los Angeles freeway. This constituted a relatively high proportion of all 700 of the 1955 Corvettes built, but the Southern California climate and lifestyle was a natural market for the innovative "first American sports car." Getting a publicity photograph like this into the press was relatively easy; making arrangements for the picture was probably harder. (N.)

Corvette received major appearance changes in 1956. Shown here is a custom Corvette created for HRH Prince Bertil of Sweden, who is at the wheel being instructed by Harley Earl, the GM styling vice president. Regular-production Corvettes incorporated concave scoops on front fenders and doors, external door handles, roll-up windows, chrome-ringed headlamps, and tail lamps smoothed into rear fenders. The Chevrolet V8 for the Corvette was tweaked with a higher compression ratio to hit 210 horsepower. (N.)

Under a joint resolution of the Automobile Manufacturers Association (AMA), major automakers agreed to discontinue racing family sedans, but Corvette enthusiasts within GM could not resist racing it. Here, this modified 1956 Corvette competes in a sports car race, probably on a road-race course rather than on a typical oval track. (N.)

Chevrolet introduced another innovative body style for 1956: the sleek "four-door hardtop convertible" Sport Sedan, shown here in the top Bel Air Series. Before air-conditioning came to the low-priced field, when occupants opened the windows of the hardtop, the pillar-less expanse gave them the feel of a convertible. Annual model changes in 1956 included new front and rear appearance and new side moldings and paint schemes. Most buyers opted for two-tone coloring. (N.)

This 1957 Chevrolet four-door hardtop continued the body of the 1956 model on the previous page, but had a new front and finned rear fenders, a new grille and bumpers, a new instrument panel, and twin hood ornaments. Ford and Plymouth both had all-new bodies for 1957 and in that year, Ford had 1,770,918 new registrations, besting Chevrolet—for the first time since 1935—by the slim margin of 31,000 units. (N.)

This image shows how the 1957 Chevrolet conventional pillared four-door sedan appearance differed from that of the hardtop above. Both four-door models are shown in the upper Bel Air Series. Wheelbase continued at 115 inches, the same as the 1949 models, and the horsepower of the base 265.5 cid V8 stayed at 162—170 with Powerglide—but larger optional engines up to 220 horsepower were offered on 1957 Chevys. (N.)

These two 1957 Chevrolets were converted to 12-passenger buses for transportation in California's Yosemite National Park. They had openable tops to give passengers views of the park's towering Sierra Mountains. The image also shows the 1957 front-end styling not seen in the two previous 1957 views. Before the end of the 20th century, 1957 Chevys became the surprising champion of late-model collectible cars. (N.)

In September 1958, General Motors celebrated the golden 50th anniversary of its founding by Billy Durant. Here, posing with an array of GM's 1958 models is Harley Earl, the legendary chief of GM styling since 1927. Behind the Chevrolet Impala in front are, from left to right, Oldsmobile, Pontiac, Buick, and Cadillac, all with the new quad headlamps that swept the industry that year. (G.)

The Impala, seen in front and rear views, was a new top-of-the-line model for Chevrolet in 1958. Note the triple tail lamps on each side. Lower series 1958 Chevys had only pairs on each side. Again, the sheet metal was all-new and rounded rather than sharp-edged. Impalas came as $2,586 hardtops or $2,724 convertibles, with up to 290 horsepower available. (N.)

This is a half-ton 1958 Chevrolet Series 3100 Panel, newly branded "Apache." The southwestern model name on all 1958 trucks was probably more fitting for a pickup truck than this van. The front-end appearance had been modified from earlier models to accommodate standard quad headlamps and a new grille. Half-tons could be ordered with optional four-wheel drive and, late in the year, pickups were offered with either "Step-Side" or Fleetside boxes. (N.)

The addition of quad headlamps to the 1958 Corvette gave it an entirely new front appearance although the grille, bumpers, and fenders were otherwise unchanged. A detachable, storable hardtop had become available two years earlier as a $200 option. Factory price was up to $3,631 and Corvette's standard V8 was 283-cid with 230 horsepower. (N.)

This photograph with callouts of the 1958 Corvette instrument cluster shows the many features demanded by sports car buyers at a time when instruments for family sedans were being simplified, including the much-criticized but practical "idiot lights" for such issues as overheating and low oil pressure. The overall feel of the Corvette cluster, as intended, is that of a fighter aircraft's cockpit. (N.)

This photograph promotes the new availability on 1958 Chevrolets of a $468 dealer-installed "hang-on" air conditioning unit. Even heater-defrosters were still optional equipment ($49–$77) on Chevrolets and other low-priced cars of the time. The image also shows the awkward "knee-knocker" wraparound windshield common on GM cars since 1955. (N.)

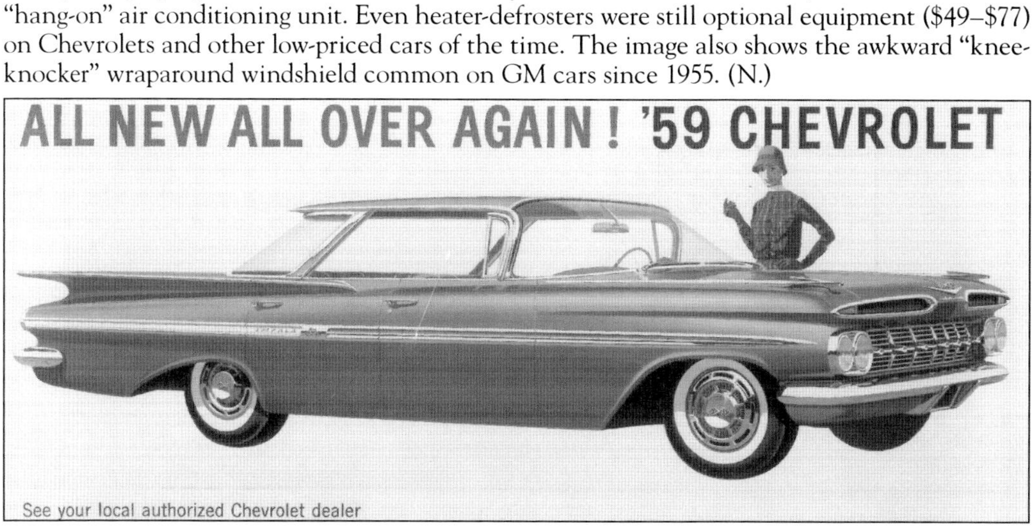

As this billboard proclaims, Chevrolet presented another all-new—and this time, radical—design change in 1959, involving panoramic vision from inside the "greenhouse," with "seagull" and "cat's eye" styling in the front and rear. Bodies were roomier; two inches wider with a four-inch-longer 119-inch wheelbase. In addition to the venerable 235.5-cid Six, the base V8 was now 283-cid, with 348-cid options offered. (N.)

The new instrument panel and wide windshield view of a 1959 Bel Air sedan is seen here. Impala was now the top series designation for Chevrolet, Bel Air the middle series, and Biscayne the entry level. Due to a steel strike affecting GM's production but not Ford's, in calendar year 1959, Ford again captured the sales crown—for only the third time since 1930—with registrations of 1,760,789 to Chevrolet's 1,721,913. (N.)

Big news for Chevy enthusiasts was the 1959 introduction of the car-bodied El Camino coupe pickup, the first such model since 1941. It was fashioned after Chevrolet's roadster and coupe pickups of the 1920s and 1930s and Australia's "utes," but was brought out in response to Ford's 1957 Ranchero—the beginning of an intense product proliferation war between the two makes. The El Camino had a half-ton cargo rating. (N.)

This view of a 1959 Chevrolet shows the exaggerated rear styling of the car. A Detroit legend held that the design evolved from miscommunication within GM. Styling vice president Harley Earl went on an extended European vacation and underlings revised his original plan, one providing easy transition to 1959 from the 1958 design. There was no question that the public recognized the 1959 Chevy as new. Earl retired in 1958, succeeded by Bill Mitchell. (N.)

In response to the 1959 Chevrolet design, underlings at Ford—or perhaps its advertising agency—produced an anonymous limited-distribution cartoon book poking fun at the Chevy. This is a selection from the booklet. Such hi-jinks between the two auto companies are indeed legendary in Detroit and continue today. (D.)

This 1960 Chevrolet Bel Air had a considerably toned-down rear-end treatment after negative reaction to the 1959 model seen on the opposite page. The front end of the 1960 Chevy was also restyled with new fenders, hood, bumper, and grille. With introduction of the compact Corvair car (next page) for 1960, regular-sized Chevrolets began to be referred to as "big," "standard," or "full-sized." (N.)

Chevrolet's half-ton 1960 Fleetside Apache C10 pickup echoed some of the hood-sculpturing design of the 1959 passenger car. In 1960, Chevrolet offered an astounding 185 trucks on 18 different wheelbases with nine different engines and several transmission choices. Chevy trucks continued to outsell Ford trucks by a considerable margin, 256,000 to 209,000 in 1960. (N.)

Introduction of the radical, rear-engined compact Corvair sedan for 1960, shown here with the Impala, was the subject of great speculation in the months before its October 1959 unveiling. On a 108-inch wheelbase with an overall length of 180 inches, the Corvair was noticeably smaller than the now "Big" Chevys on 119-inch wheelbases with an overall length of 211 inches. (N.)

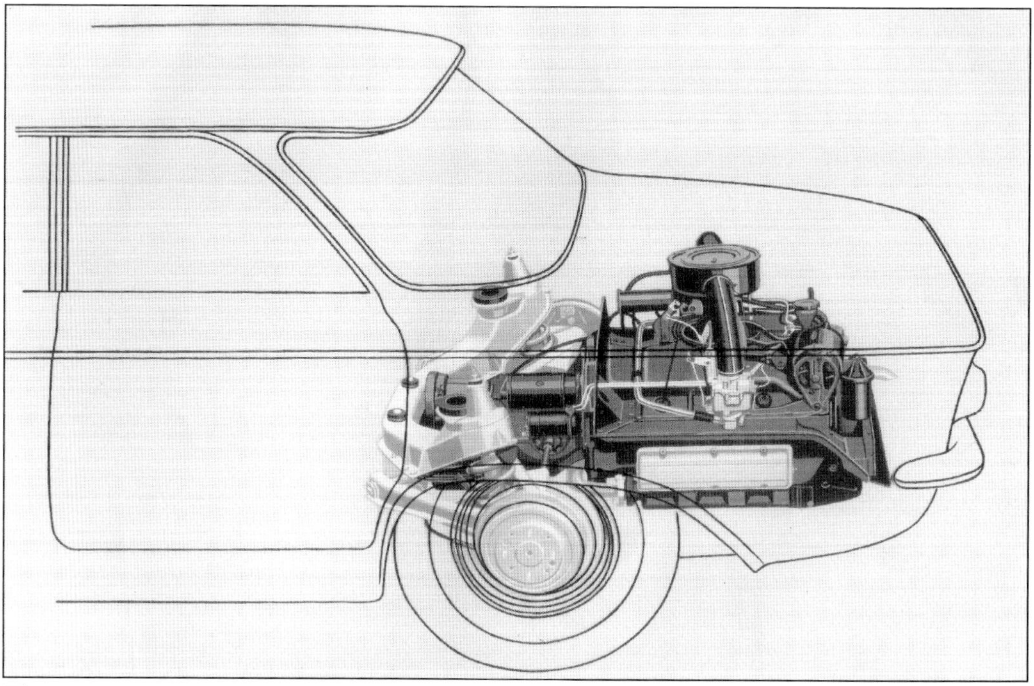

The Corvair's power train excited as much attention as the car's rear-drive configuration. It was powered by a 140-cid, 80-horsepower, six-cylinder, horizontally-opposed, air-cooled, aluminum-block engine initially shared with no other GM car or truck. This phantom drawing shows how the engine was mounted above and slightly behind the rear wheels, driven through a transaxle. (N.)

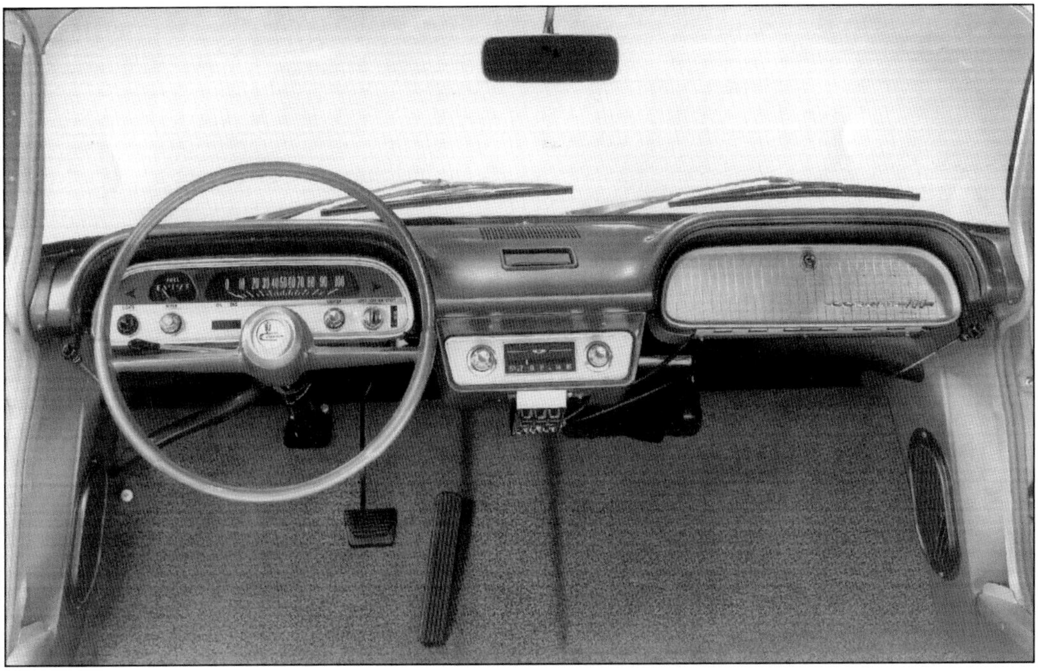

The 1960 Corvair instrument panel had a simple lever for the automatic transmission projecting from the right side of the cluster while manual shift used a floor mounting. The floor was flat in the front and rear because there was no front-to-rear driveshaft. Engineering was patterned in many ways after the German Porsche, but the car was initially presented as an economical six-passenger $2,038 family sedan rather than a sports car. (N.)

Here, Corvair's clean rear design is seen. The deck lid had louvers across it for engine ventilation and lower vents can be seen below the bumper. Luggage was stowed under what would have been the hood of a front-engine car. The rear seat also folded down for additional carrying space. Unlike other Chevrolets, the Corvair had no heavy frame underneath the unitized body. Corvair marked a suitable milestone for Chevy's first 50 years. (N.)

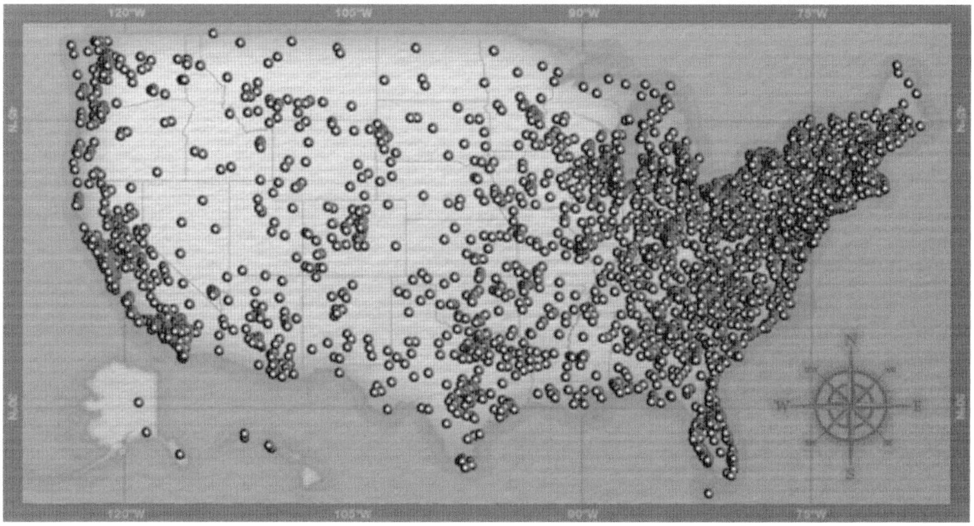

Consistent with our mission to preserve history on a local level, this book was printed in South Carolina on American-made paper and manufactured entirely in the United States. Products carrying the accredited Forest Stewardship Council (FSC) label are printed on 100 percent FSC-certified paper.

MADE IN THE USA